When I Can't Find God

DR. JOHN DEE JEFFRIES
EDITED BY C. GENEVIEVE JEFFRIES

When I Can't Find God
Copyright © Dr. John Dee Jeffries
Published By Parables

All Rights Reserved. No part of this book may be reproduced or utilized in any form or by any means, electronic or mechanical, including photocopying, recording, or by any information storage and retrieval system, without permission in writing from the author.

Unless otherwise specified Scripture quotations are taken from the authorized version of the King James Bible.

First Edition   August, 2015

ISBN 9780996616508

Printed in the United States of America

Readers should be aware that Internet Web sites offered as citations and/or sources for further information may have been changed or disappeared between the time this was written and when it is read.

Illustration provided by www.unsplash.com

Dedication

To Becky Earhardt
Who Helped Me Find God

To Dr. Buford Easley
My Pastor, Mentor and Friend
Who Rooted Me In God's Kingdom

Pathways To The Past
Each volume of our *Pathways To The Past* series stands alone as
an Individual Book
Each volume stands together with others
to enhance the value of your collection

Build your Personal, Pastoral or Church Library
Pathways To The Past contains an ever-expanding list of
Christendom's most influential authors

Augustine of Hippo,
Athanasius,
E. M. Bounds,
John Bunyan,
Brother Lawrence,
Jessie Penn-Lewis,
Bernard of Clairvaux,
Andrew Murray,
Watchman Nee,
Arthur W. Pink,
Hannah Whitall Smith,
R. A. Torrey,
A. W. Tozer,
Jean-Pierre de Caussade,
And many, many more.

www.PublishedByParables.com

When I Can't Find God

DR. JOHN DEE JEFFRIES
EDITED BY C. GENEVIEVE JEFFRIES

Table of Contents

Introduction:	A Single Tear Flowed Down His Cheek.	1
Foreword:	Commissioned by God	5
Chapter 1:	Faith and Focus	8
Chapter 2:	Faith and Frailty	13
Chapter 3:	Faith and Formulas	23
Chapter 4:	Faith and Forgiveness	31
Chapter 5:	Faith and Frustration	38
Chapter 6:	Faith and Failure	48
Chapter 7:	Faith and Feelings	55
Chapter 8:	Faith and Fear	63
Chapter 9:	Faith and Fear (Of Death)	69
Chapter 10:	Faith and Foolishness	75
Chapter 11:	Faith and Flesh	82
Chapter 12:	Faith and Fantasy	88
Chapter 13:	Faith and Facts	96
Chapter 14:	Faith and Friends	101
Conclusion:		104
Postlude:		108

WHEN I CAN'T FIND GOD

Introduction
A Single Tear Flowed Down His Cheek.

I was 11 yrs old – and an altar boy. (From "Altar Boy" to "Altar Call" – now there's a story, but, well, that's another story). I was 11 yrs old – and an altar boy. In a church. Wearing a long white robe. Lighting candles.

People, inside the church, filled with fright, were suddenly, hurriedly rushing out of the sanctuary. I heard their loud, frightening voices but I could not understand what they were saying. Then, I heard a loud sound – 'gbaam' – a small altar boy on the other side of the sanctuary carrying a golden vessel filled with incense dropped it to the cold, marble floor as he too ran from the sanctuary. A hush of horror came over me as I quietly cowered behind several pews near the front of the church.

I could hear an angry voice shouting but it seemed far away, yet dangerously near. It was a hostile demanding voice. It was the voice of a man – a man shouting angrily. In fear, people were running from the church. I was stunned, shaken, yet frozen with fear. The angry shouting voice was getting closer and closer.

"Come down from that cross.
If you are the Son of God, come down from that cross."

Above me the dying figure of Christ, carved in stone, was fastened to a large stone cross -- a huge crucifix. As I stood there, cowering in fear, looking at the hard, cold chiseled face of the man, then at the hard, cold chiseled face of the stone Christ, I felt myself shaking, rocking back and forth, filled with inward trembling and fear.

The man's eyes were wild and wide with uncontrollable rage. He stared, then, disorientated and half-crazed, he continued shouting angrily at the hard cold stone figure of Christ hanging on the cross above me. He raised one of his fists defiantly into the air to point an accusing finger toward the crucifix, screaming like a madman at the stone figure of Jesus.

"Come down from that cross. Come down from that cross."

A trembling, nervous little priest wearing a long flowing black robe came into the sanctuary from behind the altar.
"Sir, please, sir. Look carefully. This Christ is but stone. He cannot hear you. He cannot come down. He is not real."
As the priest spoke, the angry man's eyes met mine. I stood motionless beneath the sanctuary lamp, hiding behind a rack of candles – simply staring into his eyes. Then he turned his eyes away from me and began to weep.
When the priest said "He is not real" the man looked at me again then nodded his head toward me as a single tear slowly crawled down his cheek. Behind that tear was a hidden language whose meaning I did not then understand – I was only 11 yrs old. Only later, as an adult, would I see that tear crawl down another cheek -- my own. It was then that I heard the language -- and understood.
When you come to the place where nothing matters, nothing but hearing from God, and God seems strangely absent, distant, silent – then you too will hear the hidden language – the language of the heart, of the spirit -- as a tear slowly crawls down your cheek. Then you too will understand.
The presence of God is difficult to define but His absence is easy, very easy to detect. Where are the wise men? Where are the sages? Who is sufficient for the agonizing absence of God?

"Eloi, Eloi, lema sabachthani?"
"My God. My God. Why hast Thou forsaken me"

Scholars, sages, philosophers, even Jeremiah, the weeping prophet, and David, the sweet psalmist, mourned the horrid absence of God. Through their pens, their poetry and their pulpits we learn of the dismal dark night of the soul, the cold winter of faith, the dry desert journey – and other metaphors, images, symbols and motif's that describe the agonizing absence of God.
The Absence of God.
In contemporary times stalwart men of God cautioned and consoled the modern expression of this phenomena. Dr. Perry Sanders, former pastor/pastor emeritus, First Baptist Church, Lafayette, Louisiana, called these experi-

ences "God's Attention Getters." Popular preacher Ron Dunn described them as "Strange Ministers." Others, like Henry Blackaby, Experiencing God, write and speak of a "Crisis of Faith."

No matter how these experiences are described, the absence of God seems to be woven into the very fabric of life. These experiences, the absence of God, and its counterpart, the presence of God, are not, however, hollow or empty experiences. They do have a purpose -- to nudge us to seek God.

What about you? I think it would be fascinating to find out what caused you to choose to read this particular book. Perhaps you've messed up in life – I mean really messed up. And, you've done as most of us have done when we've messed up. You turned to God – but in your case you couldn't find Him. He was nowhere to be found.

Why is that? Others seem to sense God's presence in such wonderful ways – but not you. And here you are with this book in your hands, struggling to find God.

Good for you. This book is intentionally designed to enable you to understand the implications of its title – When I Can't Find God.

Know this at the onset of our journey together -- We've all made our share of mistakes. You have and I have. We've fumbled the ball. We've blown it. We've wasted opportunities. Stumbled. Fallen. Failed.

What do you do when your patience with life is worn out. Everything seems to be unraveling. The pressure is mounting. And, to make matters worst you desperately need God. You need God's help. You need God to intervene – but you can't FIND GOD.

What do you do? You're in the thick of trouble and you know it. And, you're worrying. You're worrying and you're wondering...

IS THERE ANY HOPE FOR ME
The Answer is...YES.
IS GOD REALLY HERE, NEAR, RIGHT NOW
The Answer is...YES.

Know this: The LORD is near, very near – and He hears your silent cry. He knows your desperation, your loneliness. He sees your tears, your heartbreak, your disappointment, your pain.

The Christ made with human hands -- the Christ made of stone, of wood, or of plaster, that Christ is not real. That Christ cannot help you.

The Christ, the Son of God, the Christ who is Very God of Very God, He is not only real but near, very near. He can and will help you. He weeps with your weeping – not because He is powerless, but because He knows and understands your situation, your circumstance, your anxieties and your fear -- better than you do. He understands you better than you understand yourself.

So, learn to listen. Listen now. Listen for God's voice -- hear the language – and understand – even as...

A Single Tear Slowly Crawls Down Your Cheek.

The angry man sensed an absence of God. He couldn't find God. I've wondered about him – often. I've prayed for him -- often. And, I've wondered – why was it that he couldn't find God? Why is it that there are times when I can't find God? And what should I do When I Can't Find God. This book attempts to address the struggle and deeper issues associated with that painful experience – When I Can't Find God.

Foreword
Commissioned by God

Today. Sunday. Something happened today. Something happened today -- to me – in a way that has never happened before – and I was stunned.

Goose bumps. I've got 'em even as I write.

Today, the congregation of the Lord gathered for worship. The Spirit of God moved. The people of God sang. Wonderful music. Then, preaching. Then, the most exciting part – the invitation.

Ethan. His name is Ethan. He's 11 yrs. old. Ethan came forward today. He and his mom joined the church a month or so ago. Ethan is saved – has been for awhile. I knelt on one knee to look Ethan full face. "Why are you coming, Ethan? Why are you coming?"

Ethan said something about prayer. I couldn't understand exactly what he was saying, but it was something about prayer. So I prayed – for Ethan. Then, "Amen." As I stood, young Ethan returned to his seat – and sat next to his mom.

A man then came forward. I stood looking him full face. We prayed. He then sat on the front row waiting to publicly profess faith in Christ.

Then, coming forward, this time like a determined little soldier commissioned by God to complete a Divine assignment, was – young Ethan. Once again I knelt on one knee. "Why are you coming, Ethan?"

"My mom said I shouldn't come up here so much but I told her that GOD TOLD ME to come up here again."

Goose bumps. They rose then faded quickly as a slight shudder swept through me. It was just a shudder, a tremble, sort of like an impulse, yet an undeniable impulse, almost like a chill, definitely noticeable, yet fleeting. There for just a hair of a second, then, it was gone.

I squirmed a bit, shook my head a little, then, the feeling came again. Goose bumps. Undeniable, but this time followed by a different sensation, a warm sense of peace, a sense of well being.

"God told you?"

"Yes, God told me."

I won't presume to know how you know or how you feel when you sense that you're in the presence of the Lord, or that the Lord is speaking to you, or how it is that you know that it is God you're hearing. But, deep down, from deep within, I knew I was encountering the Lord – through 11 yr. old Ethan.

"When I came forward before you misunderstood, Brother John. You misunderstood. When I came forward before I did not come to you to pray for me – GOD TOLD ME to come and pray for you."

Pause with me for a moment. Some, reading these words, are pastors. You've extended invitations and participated in altar calls. And, like me, you have prayed for others and have had others pray for you.

Question: If a little 11 yr. old boy came forward and said with total seriousness and conviction -- "GOD TOLD ME to come and pray for you." Question: What do you think the child would pray?

"Pray for me, Ethan. GOD TOLD YOU to come and pray for me. Pray for me."

And Ethan prayed..... (These were the exact words he used to open his prayer)

"Brother John, you are the Mouth of God. God wants you to fill your mouth with His Word.... God says that......"

And, what followed those initial words were prayers, pronouncements and prophecy. His words were deep, profound, powerful – and personal. A special prayer just for me from a little boy who said with conviction and certitude, "GOD TOLD ME to pray for you."

" The Mouth of God." "The Word of God." "A Child of God."

Goose bumps. I've got 'em even as I write.

Think with me, however. If a man proclaims loudly enough that he's an agnostic, he's given a book contract, appears on talk radio, and late night television – in essence he's given a platform to tell the world he's an agnostic. Strange, at least in my estimation. You see the word "agnostic" is derived from the Latin word "ignoramus."

Imagine that, a man proclaims that he's an "ignoramus" and boom –he's an instant media celebrity.

I was visiting the locked ward of a psychiatric hospital when a male patient in a straight jacket desperately called out my name.

"John. John. John."

I was shocked to see a fella from my elementary school years. "What are you doing here," I asked, "What are you doing here?"

WHEN I CAN'T FIND GOD

With tears in his eyes he said, "John. John. It's terrible. It's simply terrible. I don't know math, John. I don't know math. I just can't do it any more. I can't – and its driving me crazy."

Think about this a bit. If a man proclaims he is a "mathematical ignoramus" – he's locked up in a psychiatric ward. If a man proclaims he is a "God ignoramus" – well, you know the rest.

The Gospel of Matthew tells us Jesus sent His disciples into the world to share the Gospel -- the Good News – with a promise that He would "be their mouth" (Matthew 10:19-20). It's the same assurance God gave to Moses in the Old Testament book of Exodus: "...I will be with thy mouth, and teach thee what thou shalt say'..." (Exodus 4:12).

In writing When I Can't Find God I have labored under the same conviction and certitude of young Ethan. Like Ethan, I'm a determined soldier commissioned by God to complete a Divine assignment.

> May God Open Your Eyes That You May See His Deeds,
> and Your Ears That You May Hear His Voice

Chapter 1
Faith and Focus

    I was raised in a very religious home. My parents were faithful in their religious obligations in raising their children. Because of their faithfulness, I received a strong religious education in both elementary and high school.

    It seemed like we were always receiving religious instruction, whether we were studying mathematics, geography, or history. Everything was correlated to God. Like the other boys and girls in our school, I attended church every school day. Sometimes, I felt pushed...even so, I was always faithful in my attendance at church and tried to be a "good boy" as best as I was able.

    When I married, I don't know what happened. Maybe I didn't have anyone to push me. Maybe I was just lazy. Maybe I believed I was just too busy. I don't exactly know why, but, somehow, I drifted away, stopped attending church and lost my interest in spiritual things.

    Several years passed. My wife and I had a good marriage, three beautiful children, a new home and all kinds of stuff. But, deep down, I sensed something was lacking in my life. I didn't know what it was but something was missing.

    I didn't know that it was God...or Christ. I just had this recurring, empty kind of feeling, a feeling that there was something more. I tried buying a new car but I soon realized a new car wasn't the answer.

    One day, my son, who was attending a Christian preschool, stated emphatically that he wanted to go to the church by his preschool. The following Sunday we attended.

    After we attended, a lady from the church visited my wife and me. The lady shared from the Bible. Even though I was raised in a religious home, we did not study the Bible.

    This lady carefully explained Scripture to my wife and me. She explained how "faith" and "repentance" work together to enable people to receive the "gift of eternal life." After explaining the Bible to us the lady asked each of us if we would like to invite Jesus into our lives.

"Do you want to invite Christ into your life and receive the 'gift of eternal life?'"

I said, "Yes." My wife said, "Yes."

The lady (her name was Becky) gently held our hands as we knelt together, making our living room sofa an altar to God. Softly and sincerely, she helped both of us pray a simple prayer of "faith." I invited Christ into my heart and into my life. I turned my will and my life over to Christ. Through that prayer of "faith," God enabled me to "repent" and "turn away from" something (my sin). At the same time He also enabled me to exercise "faith" and "turn to "Someone (Christ).

While I could not explain what I had done in theological terms, I did know that I was sincere in "repenting" of my sins, sincere in inviting Jesus into my life by "faith" and sincere when I asked Him to be the Lord of my life.

There were no fireworks, no falling stars and no band played. Nevertheless, I knew, in a very real way, that Jesus had come into my life. Even so, I remember asking Becky a question,

"Is that it? I didn't feel anything."

Becky shared that I didn't have to "feel" anything because receiving Christ was a simple act of "faith" – based on the "facts" of God's Word -- not "feelings."

"You have taken," shared Becky, "the very first of many steps of faith. 'Faith' in the 'Facts' of God's Word, the Bible – and not our 'feelings' should guide us in all matters of faith, practice and life."

Know this: the Christian life begins when we place our "faith" (trust and confidence) in Christ and in the "facts" (promises) written in the Word of God, the Bible. It's that simple.

The ever popular train diagram illustrates the relationship between the "facts" (the promises of God's Word) and "faith" (our trust and confidence) in God and the promises of His Word. It also illustrates the relationship of "feelings" and their role when we "repent" and exercise "faith" in Christ.

Imagine a train with an engine, a coal car and a caboose. The engine or locomotive in the train illustration represents the "facts" of God's Word. The engine will not run if coal "faith" is not placed in the engine. Simply stated, the promises of the Bible (the "facts") will not be realized in your life if you do not put "faith" in them. In like manner, the train engine won't run unless coal is placed in the engine.

"You have taken the very first of many steps of faith," said Becky."

What was that first step? Through a simple prayer of "faith," God enabled me to "repent" and "turn away from" something (my sin). At the same time He enabled me to exercise "faith" and "turn to" Someone (Christ).

That was the first step.

Question: Have you received Christ or are you still on the road to receive Christ? Why not put some coal in the engine, right now?

In the train analogy the key is "faith" in the "facts." The engine and the coal car work properly when coal is placed in the engine. The engine and the coal car will then function as intended – with or without the caboose.

It would be useless for the caboose to attempt to pull or push the coal car or the engine. It just doesn't work that way. In like manner, we do not depend on "feelings" or "emotions" to determine our experience of God. We "repent" and "turn away" from something (our sin). And, at the same time God enables us to exercise "faith" and "turn to" Someone (Christ).

"Faith" in the "Facts" of God's Word. That's an important key. I didn't have to "feel" anything. Receiving Christ required "repentance" and "faith" – not "feelings." And so, that Saturday night I took the very first of many steps of "faith." That's where my experience of God began.

The next day came quickly. Sunday. As the worship service was coming to an end the sanctuary choir sang a song of invitation – Just As I Am. I walked down the long church aisle, shared with the pastor what had happened the night before and, with my wife, I made my "public profession of faith" in the Lord Jesus Christ.

I had placed my "faith" in the "facts" of God's Word. The engine was pulling the coal car. And then, suddenly, the caboose showed up.

I was filled with strong emotion – excited, enthusiastic -- love, peace, joy and more. I had trusted Christ. He was my Lord. He was my Savior. I was a new "babe in Christ" – "born-again" – I was "saved."

The thing I remember most following my decision to exercise "faith" and "repentance" was the new energy and the burst of excitement that came into my life in the weeks and months that followed.

In fact, I get excited just thinking about how exciting it was. I was filled with a new kind of joy, a peace, a sense of wholeness, a sense of well-being and a special kind of wonder that only Jesus can bring. Through Christ, life suddenly gained new meaning, substance, and purpose. That old feeling that something was missing, disappeared.

At that time I had very little understanding concerning the things that are written in this book. I had found God through "faith" in Christ and had no idea that there would be a time when I could not Find God.

What I did know is that I was saved. Through my new relationship with Christ I was a part of God's family, a member of His church, filled with a growing allegiance to Him and His Kingdom.

Because something real, something genuine, had happened within me, I loved Him and felt deep gratitude for what He had done to make my salvation possible. I began to go to church as often as the doors were open. I loved the singing, the preaching, the Bible studies, the prayer meetings, the fellowship and especially the worship. I began reading the Bible daily, prayed often, even tithing and going on visitation to tell others about the wonderful new life in Christ.

Many additional steps of faith have followed since I took those first simple steps. I can honestly say it has been a wonderful life. My wife and I shared a good marriage before Christ. Through Christ, however, we have both discovered what it means to have a marriage blessed of the Lord. Everyday is an adventure, a walk of faith. Its been a wonderful, wonderful life.

I cannot, however, say that everyday has been beautiful and free of problems. There is, however, one thing that you should know – Jesus Christ has always been faithful. Every day Christ is helping me, guiding me and blessing me.

Something radical happened to me and my wife in the aftermath of a simple prayer of "faith" and a simple act of "repentance." The old hymn so often sung in our churches "and He walks with me and He talks with me" is no longer a hymn. It is a way of life. He does do that. He walks with us and He talks with us.

Which begs a question -- What happened? What happened that Saturday night when I took that first step of "faith" and that simple act of "repentance" and received Christ? What did I lack, religiously speaking, before that Saturday night?

Even though I was raised in a very religious home; and, even though my parents were faithful in their religious obligations in raising their children, there was something wrong with my religious faith – its focus.

The focus of biblical faith is Jesus Christ. If you really want to experience the presence of God don't look anywhere else. The focus of the Christian faith is the person and work of Jesus Christ. Focus on who He is and what He has done for us.

The focus of my faith was on my denominational affiliation. I was raised in the "right" church. I was sprinkled with water. I was a good person. My faith was focused on what I had done. The focus of biblical faith is Christ and what He has done. It is not centered on ourselves. The focus of biblical faith is not our personal goodness or our denominational affiliation or the good things we do. No. Never. It just doesn't work that way.

Sadhu Sundar Singh was a Christian mystic in India. He was asked what he had found in Christianity that he could not find in the religions of his native India, his reply was: "Jesus Christ."

Make sure your focus is on Jesus Christ. If you ask God, He will help you "repent" and "turn away from" your sin and at the same time He will also enable you to exercise "faith" and "turn to" Someone (Christ). If your focus is on anything or anyone else, you will not find God.

Make sure that the focus of your faith and your commitment is Jesus Christ. Have you placed your faith and trust in Him? If you aren't sure, ask Christ to come into your life – right now -- today. Then take time every day to focus on Him. Read the Bible. Pray. Worship with other believers in a church where the Bible is taught and the focus is on Jesus Christ.

Your answer to the When I Can't Find God question may be as simple as receiving Christ through – Repentance and Faith. If you have not received Christ and your faith is not focused on Christ you will not find God.

Chapter 2
Faith and Frailty

In the late 1960's there was a television program called "Land of the giants." Seven people from earth in a spaceship were caught in a time warp. Their spaceship crash landed on a planet where everything was twelve times larger than on earth. Each weekly episode had these seven people battle giant cats, children, soldiers and more. Each strange weekly scenario raised an underlying question: What would we do if everything and everyone was a giant – except us?

The truth is, we live in a land of giants. In life there are things that are bigger than us. We live in a land of giants. Some of our giants stand between us and God. When a fresh vision of God is blocked from view by these giants, our human frailty grows larger.

In the Old Testament Moses came to the forefront as a frail man with a large vision of God. Moses led God's people out of Egyptian bondage. The goal? The Promised Land. Moses dispatched twelve spies to survey the Promised Land. They did. They reported that it was a great place to live – but the place was inhabited by giants – giants that they would have to face and defeat.

Again, we live in a land of giants. A plaque reads: "Don't tell God how big your Giants are. Tell your Giants how big your God is."

What giants are you facing in life? Many people in the Bible encountered their own frailty through the rigors of life. As their frailty grew larger they sensed the absence of God.

Ezekiel, a fiery prophet of God, was one such man. He stood before God on behalf of the people and he stood before the people on behalf of God.

He stands there, see him – larger than life – towering over others, a stalwart, steadfast man of God.

Strange, is it not? The first chapter of the book that bears Ezekiel's name paints a poignant portrait of human frailty. And whose face is held high as the epitome of human frailty? Exekiel.

Here, splashed across the canvas of biblical faith, is a sorrowful portrait indeed. It is the image of a lonely man weakened by a troubled heart. He is frail and strengthless. He is finite and has come to the end of his rope. And, even though he is in the midst of a great crowd of people, his people -- he is alone – seated "among the captives by the river of Chebar..." (Ezekiel 1:1).

This man, Ezekiel, saw things that others failed to see. He felt things that others did not feel. He experienced things that others did not experience.

He was a captive, taken in the Babylonian captivity. He was an eye-witness to destruction and devastation. His personal properties and possessions were confiscated. His home was set afire and destroyed. Humanity – his friends and neighbors and family – were herded like cattle to a foreign land. And, in the midst of it all his wife died – on the very day that the Babylonian captivity began.

This frail, lonely man had witnessed the collapse of everything that gave life substance, value, meaning and stability. And, his faith was disappointed, devastated. The bitter taste of spiritual and emotional despair soured, not only his stomach, but reached down into the very pit of his soul. By all outward circumstances, by all outward appearances, it appeared that God had failed Ezekiel. In the midst of Ezekiel's encounter with his own human frailty and need for God, God seemed to let him down. God was nowhere to be found.

Know this. God is real. Even though you don't see Him or understand Him, God is real. Even though you are struggling to find Him, this does not change the irrevocable fact that God is real. He is "a very present help" (Psalm 46:1) God is present, always present. God is ever-present and can be found any place, anywhere, at anytime – by anyone.

Sometimes, on dark days the skies are overcast, blanketed with clouds. Nevertheless, even though I cannot see the sun I know the sun it there. So too, no matter how dark your days may be, God, even though unseen, is still there – with you and for you – to help you.

Again, know this. There is a God. Never doubt it. To find God, it is essential that we take that first step – "repent" and "turn away from" something (sin) and exercise "faith" and "turn to" Someone (Christ). Receive Him. Invite Him into your life – now.

Ezekiel, Jeremiah (the weeping prophet), Habakkuk, Job and other people in the Bible had similar Dark Night of the Soul experiences. Through these experiences they often encountered their own frailty as they sensed what appeared to be the absence of God. Jeremiah is the penman of the probing question – "In times of trouble, why is God a stranger in the land?"

Do you feel empty, restless, lonely, lost – helpless or hopeless? Does God seem distant? Are you struggling to find God? Take Heart! Have Heart! Invite Him into your heart – now.

Hope is the Confident Expectation that somehow God is going to work things out – even when He is nowhere to be found. Hope is that sense of certainty infused by God that assures us that somehow everything is going to be OK.

Hopeless situations fill our heads with FALSE PERCEPTIONS.

    About God   About Ourselves   About Life

Know this – Disappointment with God, sensing His absence, eventually takes us beyond the things that make for disillusionment to a deeper, more resilient faith, a resilient faith that actually gives birth to a deeper sense of hope, a certitude concerning God's presence and God's faithfulness.

When you are in the midst of the Dark Night of the Soul and God seems distant and absent, it is then that we learn about ourselves, about life, about our frailty, about faith and about God.

Sometimes
    It seems as if the things of God contradict the things of God
    Take Heart! Have Heart! Invite Christ into your Heart!
Sometimes
    It seems as if the things of Faith contradict the things of Faith
    Take Heart! Have Heart! Invite Christ into your Heart!
Sometimes
    We Hope against Hope
    Attempt to embrace a Lively Hope
Then, Strangely, Hope, like a flame
Flickers, then Extinguished!
    Gone.
    Take Heart! Have Heart! Invite Christ into your Heart!
Sometimes
    When God seems distant, or impossible to find...
    Life seems cold -- and hard – empty
We encounter our frailty.
    Take Heart! Have Heart! Invite Christ into your Heart!

My name is John. You probably saw that on the front cover of this book. For a spate of two-and-one-half years (nearly ten years ago) I traveled extensively across America leading speaking engagements. At each stop I introduced myself as *Refugee*.

No. I wasn't an alien, legal or illegal. I was one of several hundred thousand people displaced by Hurricane Katrina. I lived eighty-five miles away from my church-field for two-and-one-half years – a real challenge.

For me, it was a time of contrasts and contradictions.

On the one hand I sensed and saw the movement and ministry of God in powerful, powerful ways.

On the other hand, however, there were long, lonely stretches of empty time when I simply could not find God.

One minute God was there, present, in powerful ways. Then a minute later, He was nowhere to be found.

Consequently, in the aftermath of hurricane Katrina I witnessed both misery and miracles. I saw the majesty of a world filled with God and His undeniable presence. I also saw the madness of an ugly, chaotic world empty, void, and stained by His absence.

I embraced some of these contradictory, contrasting experiences with joy and elation and others with sorrow and sadness -- and silent curiosity. Often, I wondered, "How can this be?"

Like Jeremiah I raised questions, "In times of trouble, why was God a stranger in the land."

Yet, simultaneously, like David I could rejoice because the implied answer to the question -- "Where can I flee from God's presence" -- is "Nowhere." God is with us, always, everywhere – at all times. And He will, in His great love, made a way for us to find Him.

Though I know that God is ever-present, always, every where and though I know that that He can be found, there are those times filled with weakness, weariness and frailness when I struggle to find God.

The "trump card" for me was actually a "double-whammy" – coming first, through hurricane Katrina, then two months later, in the aftermath of the hurricane.

On August 28, 2005, hurricane Katrina steamrolled across the Gulf of Mexico with fierce, violent winds and an equally powerful storm surge. The combined force of the strong winds and the rising surge breeched protective levees, pouring and pushing water into St. Bernard parish (county), flooding the entire parish in less than thirty minutes. Every building – every business, church, school, home – all were either flooded or suffered tornadic damage.

Our two story home was swallowed up by 22' flood waters. Though the church had only 3' of water, the roof was blown off and the building was drenched and completely destroyed from wind and rain.

Of the 1,464 Louisiana residents who died 163 (12%) lived in St. Bernard parish. In the immediate aftermath of the storm, dead bodies were found floating in the waters that flooded the streets and homes of St. Bernard. Several blocks away from our church 11 bodies were found, tied together with a long rope. The prevailing thought evidently was, "If one survives, all survive."

WHEN I CAN'T FIND GOD

None survived.

Trapped inside St. Rita's nursing home in lower St. Bernard parish, 35 elderly residents drowned in their wheelchairs and beds. Inside a nearby local hospital more than a dozen bodies shrouded in white sheets lay motionless.

The smell of death was overpowering, nauseous, everywhere, permeating everything.

Added to the ambiance of death and destruction were frightening reports of suicides, sexual abuse by pedophiles, thievery and other horrid stories that revealed a disintegrating social order and an accompanying collapse of the social infrastructure.

These were dark days and many wondered, "Where is God?"

Somehow, by the grace of God I found myself aligned with those who had faith in God. This was not, however, a great accomplishment on my part. God was so evident and so apparently present that I could not do otherwise.

"The church is the only body in the world that can bear the burden of this massive recovery," I heard myself saying with conviction to a television reporter. "And Christ is the backbone of that body."

Two months later, however, a different kind of storm blew into our lives. A storm of adversity that exposed hidden, deeper frailties and weaknesses.

November 10, 2005. Roughly two months after hurricane Katrine. Our Lady of the Lake Regional Medical Center. Baton Rouge, Louisiana.

"Brain aneurysm."

The doctor's words faded in and out as he spoke.

"Immediate surgical attention."

My wife and I locked eyes as the doctor continued speaking.

"Brain surgery."

Her surgery the next day lasted five hours.

"Everything went well. Our only concern is a post-operative stroke," said the surgeon.

Genny was in the initial crucial period of recovery when she began to spiral downward. She began regressing.

"Post-operative stroke," someone said. "Post-operative stroke."

We were headed for trouble. It seemed that the odds were slanted against us – and I knew it. (She didn't. She wasn't conscious). The cards had been dealt – we held a losing hand.

Age had not brought my wife to this cold hospital room, a room filled with the rhythmic ticking of devices and machines that sounded like mechanical breathing. It was an aneurysm – a brain aneurysm and a post-operative stroke – that's what brought her here.

Surrounded by beeps and whirrs of sophisticated technologies I remember how frail and weak I suddenly felt....and how alone. Alone in the world. No friends. Everyone was displaced. No church family. They were displaced too. No real friends – just a handful of acquaintances that I met in the waiting room. And God? He was nowhere to be found. Or, was He.

In the midst of that darkness, when I felt so terribly weak, helpless and frail, I remembered something a pastor friend once said: "Never doubt in the dark what God taught you in the Light."

At that dark moment in time one singular truth became a bright light to guide me....

"My grace is sufficient for you."

God originally spoke those words to Paul. He spoke them to me. He speaks them to you. When you're surrounded by darkness, in the midst of adversity, feeling weak, frail and alone – God's grace is sufficient.

Grace is a big word. I like to keep things simple. I simply see Grace as the Arms of God reaching out through Jesus to hug us and help us.

When we're surrounded by darkness, when adversity comes and we feel weak, frail and alone, we can choose our response. We choose to become anxious, fearful and weak or we can choose to become stronger as we pass through the adversity. We choose to stand tall, cast our cares on Him and rely on the strength of God or we choose to shrink back – puzzled by the whole affair.

Christmas. A long, long time ago. I must have been 8 or 9 yrs old. My family was into puzzles back then. The Christmas presents were unwrapped. Things had settled down. I was on the floor putting together the pieces of the big, giant, 1000 piece puzzle. Next to me was my brother, Glenn. He was two years younger than I. Before him on the floor were the pieces of a giant 500 piece puzzle. Across the room my baby sister, Terry, was working with one of those toddler puzzles. It had only 4 or 5 pieces – squares, circles, triangles, and stuff like that. (Sorry, Kelly and Scott, you weren't born yet).

Every now and then my baby sister Terry would get puzzled by her puzzle. She was learning that squares do not fit into circles and rectangles do not fit into triangles.

Totally absorbed in my puzzle I became frustrated as my concentration was suddenly and quickly broken. The source? My brother, Glenn.

"Hey," says he, "Where does this go?"

Needless to say I wasn't a happy camper. Here's the deal: Glenn, puzzled by his puzzling puzzle, wanted help with his puzzling puzzle – from me. Yes. From me. And, that wasn't going to happen.

You see – I was so puzzled by my own puzzling puzzle that I didn't have time to help Glenn or anyone else who was puzzled by their puzzling puzzle. I was just too puzzled by my puzzling puzzle to un-puzzle anyone else's puzzling puzzle. Puzzling, isn't it?

Isn't life sometimes like that? Puzzled by the puzzle of our puzzling lives we confront our human frailty and we turn to others who are just as frail as we are for help and guidance – they're just as puzzled by their puzzling puzzles

WHEN I CAN'T FIND GOD

as we are.

Years have passed since that puzzling Christmas. Since then I've discovered that new puzzles constantly crop up – life puzzles that reveal my frailty and my faith. Nevertheless, our life puzzles must to be solved. Part of our struggle – and our growth – is to put the pieces together. It's that way for all of us.

Someone reading this is puzzled about raising a difficult child. Someone else is puzzled by how to restore the fire in their marriage. Someone else, is puzzled about how to overcome financial difficulties.

What's puzzling you? What frailties and weaknesses are being exposed? Which one's are being denied? And, where do you go? And, where do you turn when you're puzzled by your puzzling puzzle?

Hint #1 -- If you need wisdom, ask our generous God, and he will give it to you. He will not rebuke you for asking. But when you ask him, be sure that your faith is in God and God alone. [James 1:5-6].

Hint #2 – Trust GOD from the bottom of your heart; don't try to figure out everything on your own. Listen for GOD's voice in everything, everywhere you go; He's the one who will keep you on track. [Proverbs 3:5 The Message].

Hint #3 -- [Jesus said] "...without Me you can do nothing. [John 15:5]. "How can I do this," you ask, "if I can't sense God's presence?" Answer: By faith. Remember, faith is a choice, not a feeling. Fact -- Faith -- Feeling.

"Faith says it is so," wrote Ras Rasmullen in Fullness Magazine, "faith says it is so when it does not appear to be so because God says it is so."

We struggle. We battle. We decide. The choice, the decision that we make leads us to experience either the presence or the absence of God. This brings to mind another consideration that touches upon our frailty and our faith – stories.

We LIKE stories that have Happy Endings. Whether the story is in a Book or a Movie or Real Life, We like stories with Happy Endings.

Cinderella marries Prince Charming – And They Live Happily Ever After.

The Maiden kisses the frog and the frog becomes a Prince – And They Live Happily Ever After.

We LIKE stories like that, stories that have Happy Endings.

We DISLIKE stories that have Unhappy Endings. Whether the story is in a Book or a Movie or Real Life. We dislike stories with Sad Endings.

We all understand, however, that Life and its Stories don't always have Happy Endings.

Years ago, the American public demanded that a famous American writer change the Unhappy Ending of one of his novels. He refused. The public protest eventually abated because Life and its Stories don't always have Happy Endings. That's part of life.

We DISTAIN stories that have Unjust Endings -- Especially if we are the recipient of the injustice. We don't like living in a world filled with injustice; but, we do. And we know that some stories have Unjust Endings.

Because the Human Story is FLAWED and MARRED and filled with Disappointing Stories with Unhappy Endings and Devastating Stories with Unjust Endings, we often DESENSITIZE ourselves to the PAIN that is associated with and accompanies Life in a Fallen Universe. We either See with Dull Eyes, Shut our Eyes or Walk through Life wearing Blinders. Jesus pointed out this Human Dilemma on more than one occasion -- Seeing, they do not see; Hearing, they do not hear.

Human frailty abounds. Sometimes it's apparent. Sometimes, not. Sometimes it's denied. Sometimes it's embraced. Sometimes it's hidden. What you do with frailty or what you allow it to do to you is important, very important.

Resumes. Minister of Music.

"A dozen will be in the mail this afternoon."

So said the man at the Office of Church Minister Relations of the New Orleans Baptist Theological Seminary. He handled resumes. We needed a Minister of Music and the seminary always seemed to have an abundance of high-quality students to serve on church staffs.

"A dozen will be in the mail this afternoon. But, could I be so bold as to recommend you consider an excellent music candidate, a phenomenal fellow actually?"

"Of course," says I. "That's why I'm calling. If you feel that strongly about him, then send him over with his resume for an interview."

"That's the problem, sort of," says he. "If he's to be interviewed you'll have to come here to the seminary to interview him."

"What? Is he ill or something Does he not drive? Is his automobile broken?"

"Not quite," says he. "You see – he's blind."

"Blind? Well, that's no problem. The steps of the righteous are ordained of the Lord. If God leads him to our church – if that's what God ordains, why, we'll be happy to have him."

WHEN I CAN'T FIND GOD

The next afternoon I sat across from and interviewed a young, blind seminarian. It was his first interview. We talked awhile about many things when suddenly, in the midst of the interview, the alarm on his wrist watch sounded. He very calmly pushed a button to silence the alarm and closed his eyes briefly as I continued talking.

"I noticed a few minutes ago that your alarm went off," says I. If you need to take medication or respond to that alarm, we can stop talking for a bit."

"No. No," says he with a smile on his face. "I set my alarm to sound everyday at that hour. You see, 13 yrs ago I said 'I do' to the most wonderful woman and she said 'I do" to me. We exchanged vows and rings and kissed – I set my alarm to sound every day to remember – and I pause, pray and thank God for His special gift to me, my wife."

"Everyday?"

"Yes, sir, everyday for thirteen years, four months and three days, to be exact."

There are some things you won't find on a resume. The blind man proved to be one of the finest Minister's of Music we'd ever had. He was blessed with a depth of spirit, a sense of worship – a simply astounding God-anointed young man.

There's a fundamental life lesson here – there is absolutely no reason not to pursue God's call, no matter what setbacks you encounter. Our obstacles are God's opportunities. And our frailties? They are the fodder for faith. Your faith may be weak, frail -- miniaturized. Take feeble steps, if that's all you can muster. Remember, faith is a choice -- not a feeling.

A second life lesson -- During one Sunday night service, when the Spirit's anointing was especially heavy, our young blind music minister came and stood next to me. "Pastor," he whispered, "I have a song I wrote that I think is especially suited for this moment. With your permission I'd like to play it and sing it for our people."

Awesome. Simply Awesome. God fell on our congregation that night. And the song – it had us soaring.

The physical size, the dimensions of the blind man's sheet music was interesting -- roughly thirty inches in height by twenty four inches across. The music notes he had scribbled on the hand drawn super large music sheets were gigantic. Though he was blind he could see, somewhat, out of the periphery of one eye.

One final thing about that super large sheet music. At the bottom the blind musician had written an inscription......

"Partial Obedience Is Total Disobedience."

WOW! What about you? Are you feeling weak, frail and alone? Have you let adversity and hardship beat you down?

In the aftermath of hurricane Katrina I watched as dirty dump trucks, tractors, cranes and winches tore down our old church building. As I stood there watching the building being torn down and hauled away I saw a wall in my pastoral office. Nailed tightly to a defiant office wall was a plaque with one of my favorite verses, Romans 8:28, inscribed on it: "And we know that all things work together for good...."

Through experience with God you will see that God has used every event and experience of frailty to strengthen you and your faith – to enable you to Advance through Adversity. You may not see that now, but you will.

Chapter 3
Faith and Formulas

A Question. An Unanticipated, Unexpected Question. So much so that it stunned, stumped and stopped my daughter -- dead in her tracks.

The Questioner? My 4 yr old grandson. A Little Boy. A Big Question. He was sick, nothing major – the flu bug – fever, chills and all of the aches associated with the flu – little Nate had'em all – and he wanted God to help him -- he wanted God to heal him.

"Momma," says Nate, his lower lip quivering, and tears at the corner of each eye. "Momma, will you pray and ask Jesus to heal me? I don't feel good, momma. Will you ask Jesus to heal me?"

My daughter knelt beside Nate's bed, placed her hand on his feverish forehead – and prayed, asking Jesus to heal Nate. About 30 minutes later my daughter heard little Nate crying and sobbing, his chest heaving with each deeply broken sob.

"What's the matter, buddy? What's the matter?"

"Oh. Momma. Jesus doesn't love me. Momma. Jesus doesn't love me anymore."

The little fella was sobbing. Tears were flowing. His little heart was breaking. He was not only sick in body but sick of heart.

"Why are you saying that, Nate. Why are you saying Jesus doesn't love you anymore?"

"Oh. Momma. Momma. We prayed and asked Jesus to heal me -- and He didn't. Jesus doesn't love me, Momma. Jesus doesn't love me anymore. If He did love me He would come here and heal me."

Has your son or daughter or grandchild ever come up with a question so surprisingly deep that you think you've found the world's next great theologian?

And, what about you? What about your questions? We all have questions and we all seek answers to our questions. Sometimes, in lifes more rigorous moments we lie awake, toss and turn and wrestle and struggle to find answers to our questions – Why me? Why this? Why now?

The conversation between my daughter and my grandson touched upon some deep theological questions – Existential Questions –

> Questions about God
> Questions about God's Character
> Questions about God's Ability
> Questions about God's Love
> Questions About God and Prayer
> Questions About God's Presence
> Questions About the Absence of God
> And more – much, much more.

All this and more was troubling the mind and spirit of a small, 4 yr old boy. (We had theology courses in seminary about these types of questions; but, this was not a seminarian – this was a 4 yr old child.)

At the base of all of these questions, however, is the underlying issue of the presence and absence of God.

'If He did love me, momma, He would come HERE and heal me."

Implication: God is not HERE.

Nate was in a thick of trouble, and he knew it....You may be in the thick of trouble too -- and you know it. And, to make matters worse you can't find God. Nate formulated a conclusion, a faulty conclusion. Perhaps you have too.

Here is a simple exercise that illustrates something about your particular theological bent. Below are a series of letters bunched together tightly. Look closely and you will see that the letters make a statement, a simple statement, about God. The statement that you see first reveals something about your ability to see or not see God. Look carefully at these bunched letters -- separate the letters -- what you see?

GODISNOWHERE

Some will see "God Is Now Here" while others will see "God Is No Where." What did your brain formulate first?

Formulas are actually mental constructs that we develop to help us understand and maneuver our way through life. We also create formulars in an effort to help us find God. Unfortunately, formulars that we construct to find God have the opposite effect. Instead of creating a genuine awareness of God's presence they heighten our sense of God's absence. Formulas are one of the false answers to our questions that we create when we can't find God.

Some brush aside the probing questions of children, hoping they will go away. (They won't.) Others try to give thoughtful answers. (Give it their "best shot," yet worrying and wondering if "best shot" answers are sufficient.) They're not.

These special moments when probing questions are asked by children aren't easily forgotten. They let us know something that very few consider – children, even young children, often wrestle with deep theological questions and struggle with the absence of God.

Even young children can experience a faith crisis; and, they are shaped by the experience and explanations that they formulate. (Many of your adult understandings about God, His presence and His absence are rooted in your childhood experiences – and the conclusions that you formulated as a child).

Recently a little boy, 6 yrs old, pulled me aside after church. "I want to ask you a very important question," said he. I went down on one knee so that we could see one another eye to eye.

"Brother John," says he. "Why did God give me a brain tumor?"

In theology the attempt to answer that little boy's question, or the question posed by my grandson, or other questions like these – the attempt to answer is called a "theodicy" – a word that describes our struggle to answer difficult questions about pain, suffering, sickness, disease, death, and the ability and/or the absence of God in the midst of these painful experiences.

A theodicy is an attempt to formulate an appropriate biblical understanding of these issues.

Children ask. They have many questions. Once they can speak and express their thoughts they begin asking questions -- probing questions. They ask parents, grandparents, teachers, pastors, yes, even the the kid sitting next to them in the playbox.

They bombard us with questions, big questions, deep questions. They want us to explain the world, life, God – and more.

Show me. Tell me. How? Why? Why not? Why me?

A theodicy is an attempt to formulate an appropriate biblical approach to better understand these issues.

Notice the word formulate in the preceding sentence. It's a very important word which will help us understand what's happening when we can't find God.

The child with the brain tumor was attempting to formulate an understanding of God's relationship to his problem. My grandson had formulated a conclusion, a faulty conclusion. This whole process of developing and formulating is not simply a childhood issue. We adults formulate too.

C. S. Lewis was a philosopher, a Christian apologist, a science fiction writer, an author of children's stories. He recognized as one of Christendom's most brilliant, theological minds. Lewis was a man who loved God and loved the Word of God.

Lewis wrote a book that propelled him to international fame as a Christian theologian. The Problem of Pain, the first of a series of theological works on Christian doctrine, was written by Lewis in 1940. This book dealt with one of the most vexing of human problems – the problem of pain, suffering and death.

Though the problem of pain is a fundamental theological dilemma rather than approach pain as a dilemma, Lewis approached it as a problem – a problem demanding a solution. In his tedious – but enlightening – book Lewis presents the problem and then solves it – utilizing theologically sound, biblically-based formulations. He was immediately recognized as a brilliant theologian.

Twenty years later, Lewis, a confirmed 40+ year old bachelor, fell in love for the very first time and married Joy Davidman.

Joy died of cancer in the third year of their short-lived marriage. In The Problem of Pain Lewis dealt with the problem of pain, suffering and death from a purely theoretical standpoint.

Torn by a savage grief, the grief of a mourning husband, Lewis wrote another classic on pain, a masterpiece of introspection: A Grief Observed. His writings in A Grief Observed, however, were not intended for publication. They were intended to be a type of therapy to help him keep his sanity while he passed through the crisis. A Grief Observed reveals many things, things about faith, things about God, things about life, things about death -- and things about Lewis. They also reveal his struggle to formulate a theodicy to help him better understand and cope with his wife's death.

"The death of a beloved is an amputation."

"I thought I could describe a state; make a map of sorrow. Sorrow, however, turns out to be not a state but a process."

"Feelings, and feelings, and feelings. Let me try thinking instead."

"Grief is like a long valley, a winding valley where any bend may reveal a totally new landscape."

"Part of every misery is, so to speak, [is] misery's shadow or reflection: the fact that you don't merely suffer but have to keep on thinking about the fact that you suffer."

WHEN I CAN'T FIND GOD

In the third chapter of A Grief Observed Lewis questioned the genuineness of his faith: "my house [of faith] has collapsed at one blow." He calls his faith a house of cards – more imagination than true faith and mourned its collapse and expressed fear that in his recovery he would build another house of cards that would also collapse under the weight of the next crisis.

C. S. Lewis could explain the theoretical problem of pain but he couldn't endure the experience, the genuine experience of pain, suffering and the death of his wife. What he formulated in the realm of the theoretical collapsed under the weight of the experimental.

The inexplicable is just that -- inexplicable. The incomprehensible is just that – incomprehensible. He could only touch lightly upon the wounds of life, the tender wounds of love.

C. S., in the end, found the answer....

"I need Christ, not something that resembles Him."

It takes a great deal of courage to live with or pass through suffering. It takes great faith to believe God for a miracle. It takes even greater faith, however, to continue to believe when the miracle doesn't come. And, it should be added, it takes integrity, a great deal of integrity, to observe suffering honestly. C. S. Lewis had all three – and more.

Catherine Marshall, a much-loved Christian writer, was also the wife of Peter Marshall, Chaplain of the United States Senate.

In 1940 Catherine contracted tuberculosis. At that time there was no known cure and no viable treatment, other than bed rest. She was assured by her physician that her case would require two or three weeks bed rest. Two weeks, however, became two months and two months became two years and then, finally, after nearly three years she recovered from her illness.

While struggling to recover Catherine experienced the dismal dark night of the soul. She endured the cold winter of faith and, though spiritually parched by her dry desert journey, she regained good health and a faith that flourished. (That does not mean that she didn't have challenges, or that she didn't take a few mis-steps along the way -- she did).

The philosopher Thoreau wrote that "Most men lead lives of quiet desperation." "Quiet Desperation." As Catherine's disease progressed Catherine was overwhelmed with desperation, a desperation that led her to do something that had never before been done. Without the aid of a computer Catherine worked her way through the New Testament Gospels (Matthew, Mark, Luke and John) and documented every incident of healing by Jesus. With great detail she wrote down who was healed. She listed their ailment. She also documented what was said and who said what. Did Jesus say anything? Did the person healed say anything? Did someone else say something?

Question.   What was Catherine doing – or attempting to do?
Answer.   She was searching for a New Testament healing formula.

Catherine was a product of her age – the scientific age -- the age of formulas. If you heat water to 100°C or 212° F the water will boil, every time. That's the scientific formula. Water freezes at 32 degrees Fahrenheit, 0 degrees Celsius, every time. That's the scientific formula.

There's nothing wrong with scientific formulas. They reveal the physical laws that God established to govern the temporal realm. The laws that govern the eternal realm, however, are not temporal, but spiritual. The laws of physics, for instance, that govern the physical world do not govern the spiritual world.

Mathematics is a system and a series of numerical equations, equations that are logical and work, every time. We know that $1+1=2$, every time. It always works that way. It works that way for you. It works that way for me. Mathematical formulas work, incidentally, whether you know them or not. They work every time.

You don't need to be a mathematical genius to be a formula person. I saw a book the other day – Three Easy Steps To Quit Smoking. No math was involved in accomplishing these three easy steps because mathematical equations weren't part of the process. But, a formula was. That's what the three easy steps represented – a formula – a three step formula.

Catherine Marshall was desperately searching the Gospels for a healing formula. If she could uncover the formula she could unlock the key to healing; but there was no key and there were no miracle formulas. What she did discover is that God is above, beyond our mental constructs and not bound by formulas – a tough lesson for Catherine and for us to learn.

We can certainly sympathize, even empathize, with the plight of Catherine Marshall. What that portion of her life reveals, however, is our human tendency to embrace formulas.

A number of years ago two men in their mid-thirties began attending the church where I served as pastor. Their situations were very similar. Both had recently separated from their wives. While there are always variables in situation like this, their backgrounds, circumstances and stories were remarkedly similar. They both wanted their marriages restored and they both felt that the best way for that to happen was to return to church. Church attendance, reading the Bible, prayer, and giving financial support to the church was something they both did with great regularity.

After roughly two months a breakthrough, a miracle – one of the marriages was restored. It was a time of great rejoicing for everyone – well, almost everyone.

WHEN I CAN'T FIND GOD

"I come back to church, give money, read my Bible and pray and he gets his marriage back; but, not me. I knew God didn't care about me. I knew it."

Unintentionally, unconsciously, the disenchanted, estranged husband formulated a faulty conclusion. While attending church, reading the Bible, prayer and other spiritual practices are good and very helpful – they are not the formula to resolve our difficulties (These are aids that complement, supplement and under gird resolution – not sure-fire formulas).

If there is a way that we can employ or deploy a formula that causes God to solve problems then God would be a Jack-in-the-Box God who pops in and out of view based upon how hard we cranked the magical prayer box. In essence we would have God jumping through hoops, doing our bidding, as we deploy our formulas.

And so, like Catherine Marshall, we search the Bible looking for our "Genie" in the Bible. We search for what worked for others and we categorize then formulate a formula. When the formula doesn't work we're disappointed. We then embrace faulty conclusions about ourselves, about life – and about God.

"...I knew God didn't care about me. I knew it."

Implication: If God really did care for me he would be HERE, restoring my marriage. God is not HERE.

'If He did love me, momma, He would come HERE and heal me."

Implication: God is not HERE.

Hopeless situations fill our hearts and heads with false perceptions about ourselves, about life, about God – and about how we relate to Him.

When we "repent" and "turn away from" something (our sin) and exercise "faith" and "turn to" Someone (Christ) we enter into a personal relationship with God.

Relationships are never built on formulas. Nevertheless, when the going gets rough our tendency is to read the Bible looking for formulas, steps that we might take – so that we might better crank up our God-in-a-Box. We are by nature formula people.

Sometimes, especially during life's darker days, trusting God is difficult. Yet, this much is certain: whatever your circumstances, you can trust God. The secret to moving forward is to nourish your faith as best as you are able.

Remember, there is a part that is God's that you cannot do. God will do His part. Count on it. But, know this: there is a part that is yours that God will not do. Do your part.

Those two men who so desperately wanted their marriages restored were doing the right things...and you should too: invest time in Bible study, prayer, meditation, and church attendance. But, do these things with the right motivation – strengthening your relationship with God. The wrong motivation – doing these things as a formula to get God to do something – will lead to disappointment and make God seem distant.

When we invite Christ into our lives and are born again we are born again into what the Bible calls ..."a lively hope."

This "lively hope" gives us the confident expectation that somehow God is going to work things out for good (Romans 8:28)

This "lively hope" gives us that sense of certainty that somehow everything is going to be OK....and it will be, through Christ. (I was about to close this chapter by saying, "Trust me." But, don't trust me -- Trust Christ.)

The Bible promises this: tough times are temporary but God's love endures forever. So what does this mean to you? Just this: from time to time everybody faces hardships and disappointments – even disappointment with God – and so will you.

When tough times arrive, God always stands ready to protect you and help you. Your task is straightforward – you must share your burdens with Him.

Sometimes it's hard to trust God. Sometimes, walking by faith is a bummer. Formulas are so tempting. Avoid them. Keep walking with God...and keep trusting Him.... God knows where you are and what you're dealing with at this very moment.

Where do you begin? Somewhere near you, perhaps around the corner, perhaps down the street, God has a church filled with loving people led by a kind, wise, godly pastor. They're waiting for you, your family, your children -- and your questions.

Chapter 4
Faith and Forgiveness

"You don't know me, but I am no longer dating your husband...I'm sorry for any pain I caused your family."

Forgiveness is costly. It cost something to extend forgiveness. Unforgiveness is costly too. It cost something to withhold forgiveness. The price that is paid to extend forgiveness, however, is different than the price paid to withold it.

The price paid for forgiveness is actually an investment in three relationships – God, others and ourselves. The price paid by unforgiveness is opposite -- a divestment in those relationships. Unforgiveness draws something out of relationships – it sucks the love and the life out of them. Relationships crumble and die. Marriages collapse, children grow rebellions, people are estranged and contact with God is diminished, poisoned – the heavy price of unforgiveness.

Unforgivenesss is like spiritual cholestrol, it clogs things up – life, relationships, everything.

A television commercial stressed the value of regular automotive oil changes. A mechanic was shown replacing the motor on a car whose owner did not change oil regularly. The commercial ended with the words, "Pay me now or pay me later." And, so it is with the choice between extending forgiveness or harboring unforgiveness. There's a price to pay as life moves forward. If we're not careful the pain of the past and the unforgiveness associated with the pain of the pass will exact a terrible toll and demand a payment far greater than we can bear.

Simon Wiesenthal. Simon Wiesenthal was his name. He was a young Jewish man who worked for a Polish architectural firm during WW2. Hitler's Nazis had invaded Wiesenthal's homeland. Wiesenthal was captured and imprisoned in the Lemberg concentration camp by the Nazis for roughly four years. He survived, but nearly one hundred of his relatives did not.

Wiesenthal wrote a book titled The Sunflower: The Possibilities and Limits of Forgiveness. In that book he describes a peculiar, haunting experience that occurred while he was incarcerated in the concentration camp – one that haunts him still.

Wiesenthal was assigned the job of removing garbage from a hospital for wounded German soldiers. One day a nurse asked Wiesenthal to follow her. She led him into a hospital room housing a wounded German soldier. The man's face was covered in bandages, with openings cut for mouth, nose, and ears. The man was dying.

"My name is Karl...I joined the SS as a volunteer. I must tell you something dreadful.... Something inhuman. It happened a year ago... Yes it is a year since the crime I committed. I have to talk to someone about it, perhaps that will help."

Karl grabbed Wiesenthal by the hand, holding him tightly so he could not get away.

"I must tell you of this horrible deed – tell you because...you are a Jew."

Karl told of war crimes and atrocities that he had personally committed against the Jews, atrocities that Wiesenthal said were too horrible to repeat in his book, other than in general terms.

Karl confessed that he felt a sadistic, inward sense of glee and satisfaction as he set a house full of more than 300 Jews on fire. Karl described in horrid detail the plight of the Jews as they leap out of windows to escape the burning building. Karl gunned them down, one by one, mercilessly. He spoke of his loathing hatred for and his frenzied rage that was inflicted on the trapped Jews. Then he turned to Simon Wiesenthal

"In the last hours of my life you are with me. I do not know who you are. I know only that you are a Jew and that is enough. I know what I have told you is terrible. In the long nights while I have been waiting for death, time and again I have longed to talk to a Jew and beg forgiveness from him. I know what I am asking is almost too much for you, but without your answer I cannot die in peace...I beg for forgiveness..."

Simon Wiesenthal, a Jew, remembers standing beside Karl's hospital bed as he lay dying.

"At last I made up my mind" Wiesenthal says in The Sunflower. "And without a word I left the room."

Years later, in his book, Wiesenthal, still haunted by the experience, posed the ethical dilemma – should he have extended forgiveness? In the first edition of The Sunflower Wiesenthal posed that question of whether or not to forgive Karl to 10 readers. In the current edition of The Sunflower, there are 53 responses given from various people. Some say forgiveness should be given for the victims' sakes, others that it should be withheld. Some say Wiesenhal was justified in his decision to withhold forgiveness. Others disagreed.

Someone once said that the worst kind of anger is justifiable anger. What makes it so dangerous is that it can be justified. Justifiable anger and its dark companions – bitterness, resentment, malice, evil-speaking, wrath and unforgiveness – they all live in the same neighborhood. If you do business with one, you'll probably do business with the others too. These inward hostile emotions band together, work together and together they drive away our ability to sense the presence of God.

Imagine this situation: You've been wronged, grievously wronged, and in retaliation you drink a glass of deadly poison. Would it not be foolish for you to believe that by drinking the poison the person who wronged you will get sick? That's unforgiveness. It's irrational. In most cases the offender is living happily after while the one offended is eaten up and poisoned by unforgiveness.

Many, in the grip of unforgiveness, unknowingly hold on to their pain from the past. That's unforgiveness.

Others have chosen to forget rather than to forgive. That's still unforgiveness. Forgetting is not the antidote that takes the poison away – only Christ and forgiveness can do that.

Unforgiveness has the unintended consequence of making us insensitive to the movements and ministries of God in our lives. It intensifies that sense of God's absence and can even make us feel abandoned by God. Unforgiveness separates us from God and from one another.

Unforgiveness is pointing a long angry finger at the heart of the universe, at the very heart of God Who says "I forgive." It's like pointing that long angry finger at Him and shouting "I will not make sense."

His name was Red; at least that's what we called him. I had the joy of leading Red to receive Christ. The tailgate of his pick-up truck was his altar to God. We knelt there together under a dark sky as Red turned away from something (his sin) and turned to Someone (Christ). Red repented of his sin and invited Christ into his life. It was an out of doors night baptism service when it happened so Red was baptized in a pond that night. Unforgettable.

In the months that followed Red began to grow, develop and mature as a believer. Red became involved with the teen Bible study group. In short order, however, something inside of Red began to change. He gradually became antagonistic and more of a hindrance than a help. His theology, his understanding of the Bible and his personal beliefs began to change too. Red was removed from his leadership position and involvement with the teens – and he took it hard. He began attending another church, a church that was more aligned with his unusual personal beliefs.

Six months later, on a whim, (the prompting of the Spirit of God, actually) I went to see Red. There was no reason for me to see Red. We hadn't been together in more than six months. He was involved in his new church. I was busy with our church. Nevertheless, while on visitation I decided to visit Red.

Ten minutes later I drove down a long gravel driveway to Red's house. As I turned the motor off out of the house came Red. He was jumping up and down, shouting and praising God as he ran toward me.

"It's a miracle, Brother John. It's a miracle."

Remember Catherine Marshall who desperately searched the Gospels for a healing formula. Red was reading one of Marshall's books titled Meeting God at Every Turn. The chapter he was reading dealt with the issue of relinquishment. Catherine, as you recall, was afflicted with tuberculosis. Here's Catherine's healing account....

"...after many days of struggling, I handed over to God every last vestige of self-will, even my intense desire for complete health. Finally I was able to pray, 'Lord, I understand no part of this, but if You want me to be an invalid for the rest of my life—well, it's up to You. I place myself in your hands, for better or for worse. I ask only to serve You."

Catherine called her prayer "the Prayer of Relinquishment." Part of the Relinquishment Pray led Catherine to take a fierce, moral inventory of every relationship she could recall. She began to extend forgiveness to everyone, to anyone, every where, where forgiveness was needed. Old friends, family friends, family, co-workers – individual incidents and specific people came to mind. Catherine repented, made amends when possible and sought or extended forgiveness. One by one Catherine relinquished each situation, each person, each event and episode. She made telephone calls, mailed letters, made personal visits – in essence she took heroic action to sweep her own sidewalk – as she coated everything and everyone with the Prayer of Relinquishment.

That's what Red prayed – "the Prayer of Relinquishment." When things are bigger than you are, pray the Prayer of Relinquishment. Red did just that. For Red, it wasn't the burden of physical illness. It was the burden of a spiritual illness -- unforgiveness – toward me.

"It's a miracle, Brother John. It's a miracle. Brother John, I just finished reading that chapter, closed the book and decided to kneel and pray the prayer of relinquishment. The sofa was my altar to God. I told God that I was placing myself in His hands, for better or worse – and I asked Him to forgive me for not forgiving you. As I was giving my burden of unforgiveness to God I suddenly heard car tires, your car tires, driving into my driveway. It's a miracle, Brother John. It's a miracle."

Whether unknowingly or intentionally, many hold onto their pain from the past by attempting to forget rather than to forgive -- and there is a difference. Forgetting does not take the poison away, forgiving does. Better to forgive and not forget then forget and not forgive.

Unforgiveness destroys our confidence. Unforgiveness damages our relationships. Unforgiveness keeps us stuck in the past. Unforgiveness separates us from God and from one another.

A man was telling his friend about an argument he had with his wife. "Every time we have an argument she gets historical." The friend corrected him and said, "You mean hysterical, don't you?" "No, I mean historical. Every time we fight she drags up stuff from the past and holds it against me!"

Karl Menninger, the famed psychiatrist, once said that if he could convince the patients in psychiatric hospitals that their sins were forgiven, 75% of them could walk out the next day!

Its not uncommon to lose the sense of God's presence because of the spiritual drynesss caused by unforgiveness. After describing his spiritual drought and distress (Psalm 32:4), David then writes the word, "Selah" immediately following verse 4. This is a word that beckons us to pause and think about what has just been said. David doesn't want us to miss the point. The sense of God's presence is dimished by unforgiveness.. [Pause] "Selah"

It's not easy for us to deal with unforgiveness, is it? It's like the guy who went into the Hallmark store and asked the clerk, "Do you have a card that stops short of saying 'I'm sorry' yet vaguely hints of some wrongdoing?"

It is not the nature of a human being to forgive. Our nature is slanted toward unforgiveness. Lewis Smedes, author of the Christian classic, Forgive and Forget: Healing the Hurts We Don't Deserve, noted that because we live in a fallen world we have all been wounded. Our tendency is to nurse our wounds in an effort to move beyond our woundedness. If we are to transcend our woundedness, part of the healing process is forgiveness.

Warm and witty, Forgive and Forget and its insights help us to understand that forgiveness is always preceded by wrong-doing. Not all wrong, however, rises to the level of forgiveness, in the biblical sense. Forgiveness in the biblical sense demands that the offender, the guilty party, admits wrong-doing, confesses and acknowledges their wrong-doing, repents of what they have done and asks for forgiveness from the person or people they have wronged. (There is no apology here, as is vogue in our contemporary culture. No! Genuine biblical forgiveness implies conflict resolution that reaches deep into the thoughts and intents of the human heart in an intense way that restores broken relationships, mends that which is broken and sets everyone free).

Because of the intensity of genuine biblical forgiveness, Smede stresses the need for spiritual discernment. Some incidents of wrong doing may actually be excusable. Other events may be tolerable while still others may be pardonable. Quite often when we are wronged the actual wrong may be understandable, permissible – even justifiable. Spiritual discernment is the key.

A number of years ago a church member, a lady, came to talk with me. She was upset, angry and felt slighted.

"Just wanted to let you know – I'm quitting the church."

She shared that as she was walking down a long church hallway a member of her small group, coming from the opposite direction, failed to tell her hello.

"Just wanted to let you know – I'm quitting the church."

A few days later I led a meeting between both ladies. The first lady shared that she felt slighted and terribly upset that the other lady didn't tell her hello, especially since they were members of the same small group.

The second lady replied, "I don't have any idea about what you're talking about. Everybody in this church and in our small group knows that I am an outgoing, friendly person. That doesn't sound like me."

"That's what made it so hurtful," said the first lady.

"Well, I don't know what you're talking about or when you're talking about – but let me add. If what you say happened last Thursday, well, did it ever occur to you that I might be so overwhelmed by something going on in my life that I just wasn't myself – and I was so overwhelmed on Thursday that I was unaware of you, or pastor, or anyone else for that matter. Why is it that you are so quick to think the worst rather than the best of me?"

The end result of the conversation was that the event had indeed occurred on the prior Thursday. What had transpired in the life of the second lady made everything understandable, tolerable. There was no wrong-doing or insensitivity involved and no need for biblical forgiveness. The situation just didn't rise to that level.

The Old Testament prophet, Isaiah, says that "your iniquities have separated between you and your God, and your sins have hid his face from you..." (Isaiah 59:2)

In the Bible there are three words that are closely linked together: sin, transgression and iniquity – and all three can be linked to unforgiveness. When we sin we fall short of God's glorious plan for our lives. When we transgress we intentionally step across a moral or spiritual line drawn by God. When we commit iniquity we literally twist God's commands to justify our behavior.

Unforgiveness implies that kind of twisting self-justification, a stepping over a line drawn by God, a falling short of His ideal. Remember, all three -- sin, transgression and iniquity – are closely linked and all three can be linked to unforgiveness.

Unforgiveness can be classified as a sin, as a transgression and as a twisting of God's commands. With this as a brief backdrop Isaiah is saying that "your iniquities have separated between you and your God, and your sins have hid his face from you..." Unforgiveness

WHEN I CAN'T FIND GOD

Imagine yourself living in a home that has dirty windows. You can see the outside world through the windows but you sure could see things with greater clarity if the windows were clean. Years ago a small group of us from a church where I served as pastor were helping an elderly couple clean their house. The entire house, including the windows, was dirty, filthy – covered with grit and grime. The windows were so dull and dirty that you couldn't see through them. The outside world was a blur, a dull blur.

That's what Isaiah is saying about our sins and our iniquities (including unforgivness). Unforgivness is like dirt on our spiritual windows. We look out, we look up – but we can't see God. The dirt – the unforgiveness – separates between us and God. And God's face? Hidden.

So, there you are, looking out of your dull, dirty windows, your spiritual windows, the windows of your soul, and you can't find God. His face is hid. God, however, is still there. He still sees you. Yes. The windows are dirty, but God sees through the dirt. How can God do that? From God's side He sees the windows. He sees the dirt. But, He also sees the "cross panes" – and, its because of the "cross" of Christ that we can have our windows made clean – and then see and sense God's presence.

There are many events and experiences in life, instances where we need to simply let go and move on. There is no life in the past. The past is dead, done, gone, over-with. Leave the past in the past. Forget the past. Look up. Clean your windows. Look forward. See what lies ahead. Lay aside the burdens of the past – and the unforgiveness. Pray the prayer of relinquishment.

Chapter 5
Faith and Frustration

He was one of the biggest loser's I had ever met. He was a drunk. He was unemployed. His business had failed. He was broke, no money. He was overweight and terribly out of shape. He needed a bath. The scent of his smelly, soiled body and dirty clothes filled my office with a horrible odor. He had legal problems. He was separated from his wife and a divorce was looming on the horizon. He was also homeless. His wife had kicked him out and he was staying on a day-by-day basis with his nearly ninety-year-old grandmother. His car was worn out. He was worn out. And his patience with life was worn out. I remember his words, "My life doesn't make sense." And he was right -- It didn't make sense.

Today he is clear-eyed, clear-headed and clear-thinking. He's employed in a managerial position for a large firm. He has financial resources beyond what he had ever anticipated. He is also a tremendous physical specimen – lean and muscular, well-groomed and always neatly dressed. His legal problems were resolved long ago. He has a clean slate. His marriage is restored and he and his family share a lovely home together.

His life was once very empty, lacking substance, meaning, purpose and direction. His life didn't make sense. That was more than twenty-five years ago. One of the biggest losers I had ever met.

He called recently. Just to talk.

"That was the most memorable day of my life," he said.

I remember that day well. I remember telling him, "If you forget everything else, remember one thing: God loves you and has a wonderful plan for your life."

I advised him to do the only thing he could do. Turn his will and his life over to Christ. Invite Christ into his heart, into his life and into every unfortunate circumstance that he, his drinking and his anger had created. And –he did.

WHEN I CAN'T FIND GOD

The biggest loser I'd ever met - Won - And discovered that Christ is the answer when life doesn't make sense.

> It is no secret, what God can do.
> What He's done for others, He'll do for you
> -- Stuart Hamblen

What do you do when you've messed up – I mean really messed up? We've all made our share of mistakes. We've fumbled the ball. We've blown it. We've wasted opportunities. Stumbled. Fallen. Failed. We've all been frustrated, more than once. But, what do you do when your patience with life is worn out, specifically when your patience with your life is worn out? What do you do when you're frustrated -- and your life no longer makes sense?

Many of us can identify with "The Biggest Loser" – ("I can identify with that," you say)-- but what do you do when his story is closer to your story than you'd like? What do you do when YOUR LIFE is empty, when YOUR LIFE lacks substance, when YOUR LIFE lacks meaning, purpose and direction -- and you're immersed in frustration?

(Know this: frustration, especially the kind of frustration that is so prevalent in our culture, can and often does, make God seem distant and uninvolved in the everyday affairs of life.)

That's the way the ball bounces.

Think about that little phrase. This everyday phrase is often used when someone has decided to accept the unacceptable outcome of an unpleasant situation. It's a cliché used to explain the idea that there are some things that we cannot control and once they have happened, we have to live with the results, even if we don't like the results.

That's the way the ball bounces.

Balls are suited for the games we play with them. But, what about the game of life? In reality, when it comes to the game of life we're not really playing a game. At least, not most of us. We take life seriously. And, we're troubled when the ball doesn't bounce our way.

Every human life is a tapestry of events, some grand, some not-so-grand, and some downright disappointing.

That's the way the ball bounces.

When we reach the mountaintops of life, praising God is easy. In the moment of triumph, we trust God's plan. But, when the storm clouds form overhead and we find ourselves in the dark valley of despair – when the ball doesn't bounce our way – our faith is stretched, sometimes to a breaking point.

It was nearly forty years ago that I learned a valuable lesson. The ball wasn't bouncing my way. The storm clouds had gathered overhead and it was raining on my parade. I was in the dark valley of despair – disappointed in myself, in life – and in God.

I remember driving up to our house and getting out of the car – frustrated, confused, angry with God and angry with myself. My courage and my faith were being tested to the limits.

As I walked from the car to the house the driveway was littered with toys, toys scattered everywhere. How many times had I told the children not to leave their toys in the drive-way? Heaven only knows.

I was in no mood for toys. I remember kicking one toy this way and another toy that way. And, I distinctly remember picking up a ball. In my anger and frustration I pitched the ball against the carport wall – shouting to God and anyone who would listen.

"I quit. I quit. I quit."

The bounce of the ball. Well, as luck would have it (or should I say, as providence would have it) the ball that I had pitched with such velocity was one of those "super balls". It was one of those special balls that would bounce at least ten times higher than a normal ball.

It seemed as if the ball was being flung back toward me by a stronger arm.

Wham.

The ball came bouncing back toward me with unimaginable force.

Plop.

It was back in my hands again.

In my frustration I caught then pitched the ball against the carport wall again, shouting once again, "I quit. I quit. I quit."

Wham.

The ball came bouncing back toward me again.

Plop.

It was back in my hands again.

I repeated the whole exercise over and over, several times. It was as if God and I were pitching this little super ball back and forth, back and forth, with ever increasing intensity and velocity.

In the midst of this contest with God something strange and mysterious happened. What began as "I quit. I quit. I quit." became "I won't quit. I won't quit. I won't quit."

I learned something valuable that day. Wherever we find ourselves, whether at the top of the mountain or the depths of the valley, God is there. And, because He cares for us we can live courageously.

Our muscles grow by lifting weights. A runner increases his speed by running to increase quickness. We gain an education through hours of study. In like manner a deeper, more resilient faith comes into existence as it is stretched.

The next time you find your courage tested to the limit, the next time you're angry, frustrated and disappointed with God – the next time the ball takes a bad bounce, remember this, God is as near as your next breath.

And, one other thing – be careful -- God's got a pretty stiff fast ball.

That's the way the ball bounces.

When....

When the ball doesn't bounce your way....

When those times come to you, those times of frustration....

When you feel that you're on the bottom, whether you deserve to be there or whether life has sent you a terribly cruel blow...

When the company cancels your contract or your employment is terminated, or your investments fail or your spouse walks away....

When illness requires difficult change and challenging adjustments....

When the very worse that you've prayed would never come has come and the finger of blame is not pointed at someone else – but at you...

When the sidewalk that needs to be swept is your own and no one else's and the stamp of frustration is on everything...

When the harder you try to right the ship the more frustrated you get...

What's a person to do? What are you to do? Hear the words of Isaiah, "Seek the LORD...He may be found; call on Him...He is near" (Isaiah 55:6).

I heard of a lady who had a dream. As the dream unfolded she saw three women kneeling, praying and weeping. All of a sudden Jesus appeared. He was standing behind the women.

As she stared at the radiance of Jesus, every pore on her body began to sing, "Worship Him. Worship Him. Worship Him."

She was mesmerized as Jesus walked toward and stood behind one of the women. He caressed her face as He bent over to whisper in her ear. A smile came across her face as her desperate weeping became tears of joy.

Jesus then walked toward and stood behind the second woman. He bent over and whispered in her ear – but did not touch or caress her. Nevertheless, the woman smiled and ceased her weeping at the sound of His voice.

Jesus then walked toward and stood behind the third woman. He did nothing. He said nothing. The woman continued her weeping as Jesus turned and walked away.

The lady who was having the dream called out to Jesus, "Jesus, what is the meaning of this? Why have you turned away from this lady without comforting her? What grievous sin has she committed?"

"Sin? A sin? There is no sin here," said Jesus.

"This first woman is young in the faith. She needs my touch and needs to hear the sound of my voice. This second woman is growing in faith. She needs hear my voice but is learning how to walk by faith – without my touch. And this third woman? I am preparing her for a great and mighty work. She must learn how to truly walk by faith – without my touch and without hearing my voice. She is a vessel of great honor and great faith."

A vessel of great honor? A vessel of great faith? And the touch of God? Absent. And the voice of God? Silent.

One word describes the underside, the human side, of this type of spiritual experience, frustrating. And there is the fly in the ointment – frustration has the potential to make God seem distant; yet, God uses frustration to accomplish the opposite, to draw us near that we might experience His presence.

When such is our experience we would do well to recall that "God's ways are not our ways and God's thoughts are not our thoughts." We see things one way – God sees things differently.

History has preserved the insightful poem, The Prayer of an Unknown Confederate Soldier, to illustrate this truth...

> I asked God for strength that I might achieve.
> I was made weak that I might learn humbly to obey.
> I asked for health that I might do greater things.
> I was given infirmity that I might do better things.
> I asked for riches that I might be happy.
> I was given poverty that I might be wise.

WHEN I CAN'T FIND GOD

I asked for power that I might have the praise of men.
I was given weakness that I might feel the need of God.
I asked for all things that I might enjoy life.
I was given life that I might enjoy all things.
I got nothing that I asked for, but everything I hoped for.
Almost despite myself, my unspoken prayers were answered.
I am, among all men, most richly blessed.

Chuck Colson served as Special Counsel to President Richard Nixon from 1969 to 1973. Colson, known as President Nixon's "hatchet man" was one of the Watergate Seven. He pled guilty to obstruction of justice and was incarcerated in a federal prison in Alabama.

In prison Colson "repented" and "turned away from" something (his sin) and exercised "faith" and "turned to" Someone (Christ). This was no "jailhouse conversion." Colson experienced a radical life-change, became an Evangelical Christian leader and founded Prison Fellowship International.

While in prison Colson reflected on his life before prison. He recalled the many honors he had received, the many prestigeous court cases he had won and all of the prominent private and government positions he had held – and the great American dream that he had fulfilled.

Then it all came crashing down. And with the crash came wave after wave of frustration.

In the midst of an episode of unbearable frustration God intervened. The God who seemed so distant and absent for most of Colsons life was suddenly very near, enabling Colson to exercise "faith" and "repentence" – Colson was saved. His frustration disappeared.

God, in His infinite wisdom and grace brought serenity and success out of Colson's frustration and failure.

When life is chaotic and frustrating think about Chuck Colson and Forrest Gump, yes, Forrest Gump. In the movie that bore his name Gump was portrayed as slow-witted, as a young man not gifted with great intelligence. Nevertheless, Gump understood that life is not just a random roll of the dice. God has a plan and a promise for those who believe. With that simple understanding, an understanding that chased away frustration, Forrest placed his future in God's hands because God has a better plan.

Corrie ten Boom was a Dutch Christian who helped many Jews escape the Nazi Holocaust during World War II. When the Nazis invaded the Netherlands she was imprisoned for her underground activities. Her most famous book, The Hiding Place, describes the ordeal and the many frustrations that were linked to and flowed out of that ordeal. Irrespective of how frustrating life was Corrie ten Boon had the wisdom to conclude that we should, "Never be afraid to trust an unknown future to a known God."

DR JOHN DEE JEFFRIES

We often experience frustration when the struggle to achieve something significant proves to be more challenging than anticipated. We experience even greater frustration when we fail to achieve or accomplish significant goals.

In Greek mythology Sisyphus had the frustrating task of rolling an immense boulder up a hill, only to watch it roll back down just as it neared the top. Sisyphus then started back down the mountain to retrieve the bolder to push it up the hill again. Releasing frustration was something that Sisyphus could not do – but we can.

Acknowledging frustration is simple -- managing frustration and the distance it creates between us and God is the greater challenge.

Even though faith is stretched through the struggle, the accompanying frustrations often block out our sense of God's presence.

The prophet Habakkuk also experienced frustration and the accompanying frustrating absence of God. "Lord", he cried, "how long shall I cry for help and you will not hear?" (Habakkuk 1:2).

Habakkuk discovered that faith is not only about victory. It is also about the struggle that leads to victory, a struggle that challenges faith as we travel across life's rough stretches – stretches that are often filled with frustration.

Many years ago while attending Bible College I was frustrated, very frustrated. (Strange how what was so terribly frustrating then is forgotten today). Nevertheless, I was frustrated.

Often, in the midst of faith's contest with frustration, hard questions are asked. In essence that's what Habakkuk's prophecy is about, hard questions and tough answers.

In my circumstance back then I remember sitting in a classroom, not paying any attention to the professor's lecture. I was in a silent conversation (argument) with God. In the midst of my conversation with God I saw a crumpled sheet of yellow legal paper under a nearby vacant desk. I picked it up, uncrumpled it, and read the following, hand-written note....

> "God often takes away our comforts and our privileges in order to make us better Christians. He trains His soldiers, not in tents of ease and luxury, but by turning them out and using them to forced marches and hard service. He makes them ford through streams, and swim through rivers, and climb mountains, and walk many a long mile with heavy knapsacks of sorrow on their backs. Well, Christian, may not this account for the troubles through which thou art passing? Is not the Lord bringing out your graces, and making them grow? Is not this the reason why He is contending with you?"
>
> -- Charles Haddon Spurgeon; Morning & Evening

Years later I discovered that Charles Haddon Spurgeon was the author of the message scribbled on that crumpled sheet of yellow legal paper under a nearby vacant desk. (Spurgeon may have originally written the statement, but you'll never convince me, however, that God didn't put it under the desk.)

There are times when questions need to be asked, when doubts need to be expressed and frustrations need to be faced.

In Habakkuk's time the frustrating absence of God prompted Habakkuk to ask questions that he felt needed to be asked, questions that weighed heavily on his spirit and his mind. And God answered those questions. God said to Habakkuk, "I am going to do something in your days that you would not believe, even if you were told" (1:5).

When I sat in the Bible college classroom reading the message scribbled on an crumpled yellow legal paper I recalled that God said to Habakkuk "I am going to do something…"

God said to me, "I am doing something…" Habakkuk resolved his frustrations by focusing on what God would do in the future. I resolved my frustrations by focusing on what God was doing in the present.

The book of Habakkuk documents one man's journey from frustration to faith. He had questions. He sought answers and he was prepared for the possibility that his questions would not be answered.

God didn't send Habakkuk a crumpled yellow sheet of paper with a message on it – but He did send an answer to his prayer. And, God will hear and answer your prayers too.

I can appreciate the frustration Charlie Brown has in the Peanuts cartoons. Like the one where Lucy is philosophizing and Charlie is listening. As usual, Lucy has the floor, delivering one of her lectures.

She say, "Charlie Brown, life is a lot like a deck chair. Some place it so they can see where they're going. Others place it to see where they've been. And some so they can see where they are at the present."

Charlie Brown sighs and says, "I can't even get mine unfolded."

More than a few of us can identify with Charlie Brown. Life gets rough at times. Some of the choices we have to make are difficult. We find ourselves, like the old saying, "between a rock and a hard place" -- Stuck between two possibilities where an argument can be made for going either way. We have a name for this type of situations – dilemma.

Whenever we're faced with a dilemma we're pulled in two different directions. We feel the frustrating strain and we don't quite know whats the best thing to do. And, I might add, being older and wiser doesn't mean that you're immune to the problem.. As Charlie Brown put it, there are times when we find if difficult to get our deck chair unfolded.

When we encounter a dilemma and we're unable to figure out the right direction, it's very important that we turn to God's Word for guidance – we need to hear His voice.

There are a lot of different voices all around us, trying to pull us in different directions. Some voices are loud, some are persuasive and a few are downright convincing. It can be confusing. If you listen long enough to the wrong voices you may be tempted to throw your faith to the wind, look out for number one and make a wrong choice.

So, here's a good place to start. Go to the Word of God, pray, read James 1:5, then allow God to lead you. He will. Count on it.

Here's another bit of wisdom that can help you manage frustration. It's a simple prayer written by a theologian-philosopher, Reinhold Niebuhr. It's called the Serenity Prayer...

"God grant me the serenity to accept the things I cannot change; courage to change the things I can; and wisdom to know the difference."

In one-on-one counseling situations I often give the following written assignment: break down and write out the Serenity Prayer, a word or a phrase at a time, clarifying the meaning of the prayer for you.

After the assignment is completed I then offer the following for consideration.

- ☒ Serenity is the opposite of frustration.
- ☒ Serenity is not cranked up but granted as a gift from God.
- ☒ Even though serenity is a gift that is given, it is also a goal that must be gained.
- ☒ Even though the goal must be gained, it is still, nevertheless, a gift that must be accepted, received by faith, when God grants it.

The whole of this process is a cooperative ministry, a cooperative ministry between us and God. The process is built on a collaborative process – there is a part that is God's that we cannot do (God will do His part) and there is a part that is ours that God will not do (We must do our part). As this collaborative process matures we make an awesome discovery -- there are some things that we cannot change.

We cannot change other people. We cannot change the past and we cannot change the pain we attach to certain places where unpleasant events happened.

Because this process is so delicate and difficult, God will grant us courage to change the only thing that we really have the power to change – ourselves.

Far too often we spend too much time and energy trying to change others or we deconstruct the past or deploy other defense mechanisms to protect ourselves from the pain of the past. Sometimes we take the opposite approach and acquiesce or cower in fear, falsely believing that we are powerless and helpless. Either approach reveals a lack of emotional courage to change the only thing we can change – ourselves.

The final portion of the Serenity Prayer focuses on wisdom, the wisdom to know the difference between the things that can and the things that cannot be changed. There is a challenge here. It is simply this. The Scripture describes our sinful tendency to "do that which is right in our own eyes" – guided by our own wisdom.

The Bible states with emphasis that "if any of you lacks wisdom, flet him ask of God, who gives to all liberally and without reproach, and git will be given to him." (James 1:5)

Know this: The LORD is near, very near – and He hears your cry. He knows your heart. He sees your tears, your heartbreak, your disappointment, your pain and your frustration.

So hold on to your dreams. Hold on to your destiny. Don't give up. Don't turn back. Continue to run with patience the race that is before you.

Christ will feed your hunger. He will satisfy your thirst. He feels and is touched by your weeping, by your anguish of heart, by your frustrations. He gathers your tears in His bottle and records them in His book. You are loved. You are remembered in heaven at the throne of God Himself (Psalm 56:8)

And, remember this: when the ball takes that frustrating kind of bounce – forget about the ball – and focus on God. The mind that focuses on God shall find perfect peace -- the opposite of frustration. (Isaiah 26:3)

Chapter 6
Faith and Failure

Success, the pearl of great price in our modern, technological society, is a fragile thing. Delicate. So too are choices -- and the consequence of our choices.

Just ask Vino. Sweet Vino. Once, long ago, he lived. Now he's dead. No one lays flowers on his grave. No one knows where it is. He simply lies there, somewhere, in an unknown, unnamed grave in the Holt Cemetery, a potter's field for the poor in New Orleans.

Lingering and limping through memory – as he did through life – he turns and looks at me. I see him as I saw him as a child -- as an old man, an old man with missing fingers who walked on the side of his crippled foot, limping through life. And now, the dead Vino, the old man who once lived and worked in his studio above the Old Shanty, a neighborhood bar on Washington Avenue in New Orleans – he turns and looks at me.

"I remember you," says I in the midst of silent memories. "I remember you."

Vino was an artist and a prominent European classical sculptor. Marble. Marble was his clay. He saw, chiseled and shaped beauty, freeing it from large slabs of raw marble harvested from the earth. Many of his greatest works, noble statues of men and women of God, stand in European cathedrals – a mute testimony to a man who once lived – a man who now lies buried, somewhere, in an unknown, unnamed grave in the Holt Cemetery.

"Vino died the other day," says mom. "They found him lying on his studio floor – his face half eaten away by rats."

Marble was his clay. Alcohol was his nemesis. First the man takes a drink – then the drink takes the man. Alcohol had taken Vino where he didn't want to go. He became what he never thought he would become. Vino discovered the hard way that success is a fragile thing. Delicate.

Were it not for alcohol he would have been a wealthy man, a man of renown, an acclaimed man of high culture. Instead, he was scammed out of his money and out of his works by shrewd art dealers and self-serving investors.

In a drunken stupor he stumbled and broke his ankle and, when he finally sobered up it was too late to reset it – and so he walked with a limp. No one knows if it was alcohol or anger that led him to chisel off several of his fingers. One day they were there – the next, they were gone. And so was his opportunity for success in life. And now Vino was dead.

"Vino died the other day," says mom. "They found him lying on his studio floor – his face half eaten away by rats."

Success. Failure. Faith. There's a thin line that divides all three. To cross from one to the other is no guarantee that all will go well; or that all will go wrong. But, sometimes things do go wrong. Sometimes we fail – and, we feel alone and wish for better days. We wish we could turn back the clock. Remake a decision. Retrack harsh words. Start again. We wish, wish, wish. Do you ever wish?

Do you ever wish? Do you ever wish life had a "redo" feature? My word process has one. If I make a typographical error I can use the "redo" feature to "undo" the mistakes I've made. If something goes awry, I just use the "redo" feature.

Do you ever wish life had a "redo" feature?

My computer has a "restore" feature too. If things get so terribly messed up I can use the "restore" feature to take my computer backward in time to an earlier time before things got messed up.

Do you ever wish life had a "restore" feature?

When I was younger I used to play golf. I wasn't much of a golfer. Sometimes the ball would fly this way, sometimes that way and, more often than not – simply go astray. A "mulligan." A "mulligan" carries the same idea as the "redo" and "restore" features on the computer. You get a second chance. You disregard the errant shot. No penalties. No consequences. Simply take the shot over.

Do you ever wish life would give you a "mulligan?"

I think all of us can look backward with regret – over things we've done or over things we've said. And, we wish life would provide a "redo" feature, or a "restore" feature – we wish life would give us a "mulligan."

Bad News –– Life doesn't work that way.

Good News – God Does.

God is the God of second chances. God, through the work of Jesus Christ on the Cross, not only forgives our sins -- He actually "cancels" our past.

Many people struggle to move forward in life. At some point they seem to make forward progress. Then, inexplicably, the long arm of the past grabs them and pulls them backward. They're suddenly overwhelmed and stymied by feelings of embarrassment, deep feelings of guilt, shame, regret and more.

These dark feelings rush to the surface and when they do – we're shattered – and stuck.

>Into our Shattered Lives
>Jesus "Restores" our Hearts.

>Into our Shattered Families
>Jesus "restores' our Homes.

>Into our Shattered World
>Jesus "restores" our Hope.

When we look backward at some of the situations we have been involved in and some of the choices we have made, we often think, if only I had a second chance.

Sometimes when we make a mistake in life it feels so final. You may think it's all over for you; but, know this – God is a God who provides that much needed second chance.

There's a new day coming. Our past failures are not final and our pain need not be fatal. Know this -- your yesterdays don't always have to determine your tomorrows.

In the Bible book named Numbers, chapter 13, Moses sent out 12 spies, one from each tribe. Their mission was to evaluate the opportunity for success if the Israelites were to engage in war to gain the Promised Land. Caleb and Joshua, who were 2 of the 12 spies, brought back a good report about the land and their opportunity to conquer it. The other 10 spies brought back a bad report.

The people made an unwise choice – they doubted God, declined the opportunity and failed to enter the Promised Land. As a result of their failure the Israelites wandered for 40 years in the desert before entering the Promised Land.

An entire generation failed to make it. They failed themselves, failed one another, failed their children – and failed God. Only Caleb and Joshua, who brought back good reports about the land lived long enough to eventually enter the Promised Land.

For Caleb and Joshua, Success was their Destiny -- but, their Destiny was Delayed. For the 10 spies and the people of Israel who failed to trust God. Destiny was Denied. Destiny was Deferred, however, to the next generation who entered the Promised Land 40 yrs later.

Success was their Destiny. Failure was their fate.

Destiny Delayed. Destiny Denied. Destiny Deferred. The desert winds sang a song, a sad and sorrowful song as the people of God wandered aimlessly for forty years. The dry whisper of failure, with its unseen wings, knew nothing of success – and neither did God's people.

Success is a fragile thing. Delicate. So too are choices -- and the consequence of our choices.

We often experience frustration, as shared in the previous chapter, when the struggle to achieve something significant is more challenging than anticipated. We experience even greater frustration when we fail to achieve or accomplish anticipated goals.

We're not created to fail – or to be defeated. God didn't create us to limp through life. Victory is the expectation God has for every believer. God has saved us to be over comers. Conquerors. Victors. This is our birthright as members of God's family.

God saved us to experience Victory Over Self. Victory Over Sin. and Victory Over Satan. But, what about Victory Over Situations – especially the unchangeable kind. What about victory over circumstances that you cannot control?

There are basically two types of circumstances: (1) Those which we can control; and, (2) Those which we cannot. Being a Christian does not grant us immunity from either type. Nor does victory in Jesus elevate us above some of the more dire circumstances of life.

Even so, we are not powerless. We still have choice – and choices demand courage. God gives strength to the strengthless; help to the helpless; and, hope to the hopeless.

Failure has the opposite effect. It saps our strength, discourages and deflates, creates feelings of helplessness and blinds us to the hope that is available through Christ.

A few years ago a popular song was titled "Bridge Over Troubled Waters." Someone in the Christian community "Christianized" that song by altering the lyrics to indicate that Jesus was the "Bridge" over troubled waters. It was a beautiful song – but it was theologically incorrect.

Jesus is not a "Bridge" over troubled waters. Jesus is our Pathway THROUGH troubled waters. Remember, Jesus said, "I am the Way..." [the Pathway.] He will make away when there is no way – He is our Pathway through troubled waters.

There are some circumstances we hate to go home to, but we must. We would give anything to change these circumstances – but we can't. We have prayed and prayed for God to change our circumstances – but He hasn't.

Think about several one-word descriptions that describe how people that you know approach the unchangeable circumstances of life. If it will help you focus, write the descriptions down. (Hint: Some approach unchangeable circumstances with Anger, for others its Fear, or Anxiety, or Despair, etc). With which of these one-word descriptions do YOU most identify? Why?

Next, draw inner strength and courage from Romans 8:28 – "And we know that all things work together for good to them that love God, to them who are the called according to his purpose."

Notice the word "know" – Paul is saying he "knows" what he "knows" based on prior experience with God. The knowledge that he has wasn't learned in a classroom, but through and by personal experience with God.

Notice next that Paul says – "....we know...." We – all of us through our relationship with God through faith in Christ -- gain this kind of knowledge in the same way – through experience, personal experience with God. That experience with God gives us the kind of knowledge that Paul is writing about – the kind that gives us a strong sense of certitude, confidence, and conviction as we forge ahead through both changeable and unchangeable circumstances.

Take heart. Have courage. You're on that road, the road that leads through both changeable and unchangeable circumstances. Allow God to create in you that sense of certitude, confidence, and conviction as you continue your life journey with Him.

Notice also that "God works ALL things together for GOOD..." Paul is not saying that all things are GOOD in and of themselves. He does say, however, that God is "working" ALL things – even the uncomfortable things, even the not-so-good things, even the unpleasant, unchangeable things of life – He is working ALL things together for GOOD – an eternal good that is rooted in the daily experiences of everyday life.

While the search for success is often elusive the attainment of success has pitfalls too. Often, when we fail to attain success God will seem absent. The attainment of success can also diminish our ability to experience God's presence.

The distance between a success and a failure is only one step, and often only a short one at that. One sad truth of life in a fallen world is that we can be riding high on the cloud of success and then suddenly find ourselves in a valley, a valley of failure that creates a feeling of distance from God.

Elijah's success was followed by failure

The thrill of his victory on Mt. Carmel was quickly replaced by deep feelings of failure. One moment we can be like Elijah standing victoriously, basking in the glory of success and the next moment, we're shriveled up, surrounded by darkness, hiding in a cave complaining to God -- failure.

One of our Greatest Fears is the
Fear of Failure.

One of our Greatest Pains is the
Pain of Regret.

WHEN I CAN'T FIND GOD

Here are some "Mini-Messages" that ministered to my friend -- "The Biggest Loser" – hopefully, they'll help you too.

Remember, Christ is the answer when life doesn't make sense.

1) No matter how far you've fallen, you're not a failure. Failing is an experience, an event – not a person. Failure is something that happens, an incident. Let me reemphasize -- Failure is never a person. You are not a failure. Your marriage may have failed – but you are not a failure. You may have had a financial failure – but you are not a failure. You may have had a failed business – but you are not a failure. Your children may not have turned out as you would have liked – but you are not a failure. You may have experienced failure, but that doesn't make you a failure. You are not a failure.

2) The normal response to events of failure is –remorse. Remorse IS a natural, normal response. If you're not careful, however, remorse will produce depression, despair and other dark emotions that have the potential to lead you to...

- Project your failures onto others
- Project your failures onto yourself
- Believe that other people are horrible
- Believe that you're a horrible person
- Believe that everyone is against you
- Believe that the world is against you
- Justify and Rationalize your failures
- Even deny the reality of your failures

3) The appropriate response to events of failure is – repentance. When we repent we accept responsibility for the event. If we've made mistakes, unwise decisions and poor choices – we acknowledge that – and we deal with the consequences. Remorse is looking backward at the event of failure. Repentance is moving beyond the failure -- moving forward. Don't let the shadow of past failures cast a darker shadow on your future. You can't say you want things to be different if you're not willing to do things differently –that's repentance.

4) If your failure is rooted in sin –definitely repent, in the biblical sense of the word – and make amends wherever and whenever necessary.

- Remember, "If we confess our sins, he is faithful and just to forgive us our sins, and to cleanse us from all unrighteousness" (1 John 1:9).

- Remember, "...If our conscience condemns us, we know that God is greater than our conscience and that he knows everything. (1 John 3:20).

- Remember, what has happened has happened. You can't unscramble eggs. You can't "un-sin" sin. You can't change the past.

- Remember, you are not what you did. You are who God says you are – forgiven.

It is never too late to do what God wants you to do. This may be a dark chapter in your life; but, remember – your story's not over.

Remember...
Christ is the answer when life doesn't make sense.

The Wounded Healer is a brief biography of the late J. B. Phillips. In the midst of his life story was a prayer that he had prayed. When I read that particular prayer the Holy Spirit pierced my heart. He literally gripped me, seized my attention and led me to claim that prayer and make it my own.

I have prayed and do pray that prayer often with the conviction that its answer in my life and in the lives of God's children is the great need of the hour. I choose to call that prayer , though J. B. Phillips did not label it such, "The Reality Prayer." It is a very short, very concise, very simple prayer and I pray that the Holy Sirit will use it in your life as you follow Jesus:

"God, Help me to see the world as it is;
myself as I am; and, Thou as Thou art."

I really believe that God is genuinely pleased when His people pray that kind of prayer. It is a prayer for truth; a simple request for the ability to understand; for discernment; for wisdom; for the gift of seeing reality unencumbered by the many illusions that distort our perceptions, cloud our understanding and hinder us in our pilgrimage through this world. Pray that prayer and pray it often. God will hear and He will bless you. Now, discern this....

> No matter how far you've fallen, you're not a failure.
> Failing is an experience, an event – not a person.
> God will never leave you, nor forsake you
> Especially in your hour of need or
> In your time of failure.

Chapter 7
Faith and Feelings

In the shadows – near the rough edge of ministry – every pastor hears the faint echo of yesterday and he sees the fading faces of those who languished in the darker valley's of life.

Many years ago a man named John was forced to deal with a tragedy that was far greater than he could bear. The wounds of life, the wounds of love – and a pain so deep, so very, very deep, and so great – these were flung upon him. A large commercial airliner fell out of the sky on his home. He suffered the death of his young daughter. She was a child, his precious child.

John couldn't explain it – it was inexplicable. He couldn't comprehend how such a thing could happen – it was incomprehensible. And, he couldn't make sense out of the insensible – it was irrational, illogical. He could only touch lightly upon his wounds, the wounds of love as he felt and morned the loss of his child.

"I'm like a man walking through life with no feet," said John. "I'm alive – but I'm hurting every step of the way."

The wounds of life, the wounds of love – Sometimes they inflict a pain so severe, so very, very deep, and so great and grievous that words fail us.

Standing in yesterday's dim shadow near the rough edge of memory and ministry is another. She was a deaf mute who was suddenly and heroically facing something far more grievous that her disabilities. She was dealing with the inexplicable -- the incomprehensible – the irrational. A New Orleans police officer solemnly stood at her door. Her son, her only son – "He was a good boy, Brother John, he was a good boy."

Murder. Murdered on the streets of New Orleans.

It was – unanticipated – unexpected – she simply turned a corner in life and there it was – a pain so deep, so very, very deep – far greater than she could bear.

"Brother John, my heart; O, my heart; my heart is so torn, so torn apart, so picked to pieces," she said through sign language, "O Brother John, I doubt even God can put the pieces together again."

The wounds of life, the wounds of love – Sometimes they inflict a pain so deep, so very, very severe, and so great that poets and philosopher's and others who think deeply about such things are stunned to silence.

"Pastor John." She cried another lady, softly, so very softly – yet her pain was great, so very great – unbearable. It was an accident – unanticipated – unexpected – she simply turned a corner in life and there it was – a pain so deep, so very, very deep, and so great. It hurts. It hurts. Why did this have to happen?

> Why? Why? Why?
> Why me? Why now? Why this?
> Why? Why? Why?
> The stories change – but not the pain.

The situations that stretch faith most are those that cause life to fall apart. Our feelings are raw – God seems distant and difficult to find. How do you see God when your eyes are clouded by tears.

Inexplicably, in one day an Old Testament man named Job lost everything -- family, business, possession, health – Job lost it all. To add to his burden, for thirty-seven chapters -- God was silent. God seemed to be absent.

When you're wounded, hurt – and your feelings are raw – and your faith is stretched....

Talk to God. Tell Him exactly what you're feel.

Empty your bucket. Pour out your heart. Unload every emotion that you're feeling. That's what Job was doing when he said, "I can't be quiet! I'm angry and bitter. I have to speak!" (Job 7:11, TEV).

Job cried out, even when God seemed distant and nowhere to be found: "Oh, for the days when I was in my prime, when God's intimate friendship blessed my house." (Job 29:4, NIV)

God can handle your doubt, your anger, your fear, your grief, your confusion, your raw feelings and your questions.

Read that again...

God can handle your doubt, your anger, your fear, your grief, your confusion, your raw feelings and your questions.

Along with a successful music ministry, Del Way serves as Pastor of Calvalry Temple Church in Kerrville, Texas. He wrote and sang a song titled "Jesus Is Your Healer" – the full lyrics of that song are most appropriate at this juncture...

> Jesus Understands
> What You're Going Through
> He's Been Touched With Every Feeling
> That's Touching You

WHEN I CAN'T FIND GOD

He Bore Stripes Upon His Back
So He Could Take Your Pain
Just Reach Out And Claim Your Healing
In Jesus Name

Jesus Is Your Healer.
His Power's Still The Same.
As When He Walked In Galilee
And Healed The Sick And Lamb.

Reach Out And Touch His Garment
He Will Make You Whole
Jesus Is Your Healer
Let His Healing Flow

The wounds of life, the wounds of love – Sometimes they inflict a pain so deep, so very, very deep, that even the strongest are left limping through life. Some are mere shells of what they once were.

Sometimes, we struggle and strive to make sense of the insensible – without success. Sometimes, we strain and seek to comprehend the incomprehensible – but we don't.

In the end, we simply stand there, with an aching heart. We stand and stare into the emptiness and nothingness that has come upon us. With blank faces, astounded by what has happened, we simply stand there -- astounded, stunned.

Remember, God can handle your doubt, your anger, your fear, your grief, your confusion, your raw feelings and your questions. He really can.

It was the middle of June, 2007. No AC. No money. The new First Baptist Church of Chalmette's Grand Opening was slated for mid-September. It took five years of grueling post-Katrina efforts to get to this point.

"Shut it down," said the hurricane Katrina construction leader. "Shut it down."

"Not yet." says I projecting stubborn faith.

My stomach, however, was in knots and my faith was taunt and tight as I left the meeting. Stunned, I simply stood there on the porch of the construction building – saying nothing – doing nothing.

My burden was not the death of a person – it was the eminent death of a dream, of a vision – and our church. Our new post-Katrina church building was nearly complete, but not quite. Millions of dollars had been spent, but more was needed. Thousands of volunteers had come, but we needed more to finish the project.

"Shut it down." said the hurricane Katrina construction leadership.

"Not yet." says I.
Stunned, I simply stood there – saying nothing – doing nothing.
"There he is. He's the pastor," shouted a group of college-age construction volunteers, pointing toward me. A short black man, a man I had never met, stepped out from the crowd of volunteers and spoke directly to me.... with a strange-sounding British accent -- his name was Charles.
"I too am a pastor," said Charles. "God told me to stop many times as I drove by your church, but I did not. I cannot explain why I did not. I just did not. Today, however, the Holy Spirit MADE me stop. Pastor, God MADE me stop and He told me that I MUST pray with you and I MUST give you a message."
"What's God's message," I asked.
"God told me to tell you that He will build your church."
A Word from God. The writer of Proverbs spoke of "a right word at the right time" – "a word fitly spoken" (Proverbs 25:11). Here was a Word from God through a strange-sounding West African pastor, thousands of miles away from his homeland. I was stunned. A desperately needed Word from God -- "God will build your church."
Before we prayed he showed me a photo of his childhood church in W. Africa. "When I was a boy," says he, "I and the other children would carry black rocks up the mountain to build a new church. This is a photo of that church."
The photograph was of a church made of beautiful "black rock." A second photograph had nearly a hundred W. African boys and girls standing in front of the "black rock" church.
"And these are the 'living stones,' pastor –remember, never forget, God's message – God will build your church."
The following week 70 or 80 new, unscheduled construction volunteers came from Chattanooga, Tennessee. I told many Katrina and post-Katrina stories to the group and ended by telling them about Charles, the West African pastor, the "black rock" church and the word from God -- "God will build your church."
The volunteers from Chattanooga were stunned as I mentioned the "black rock." There was a silence, a sacred hush. Two words were heard making their way across the crowd of volunteers – "Black Rock" "Black Rock" "Black Rock." Nearly a dozen or so volunteers rushed forward and surrounded me. One by one they reached into their pockets or purses – and pulled out and placed a small "black rock" in my hand.
"Our pastor," says one, "gave each of us several 'black rocks' -- prayer rocks, he called them -- before we came on this mission trip to help rebuild your church. He told us that God would let us know exactly who should get our 'black rocks.' God just let us know -- you, pastor, are to have our 'black

rocks.' Keep a 'black rock' in your pocket as a reminder. We will pray for you. God will build your church."

"God will build your church."

About four weeks later the same church in Chattanooga sent nearly a dozen AC technicians to "hook up" our AC units – just in time for the grand opening.

Today, there are folks across the country, in our community and in our church who have one of my little "black rocks" in their pockets or purses. Why? Because there is a God and He hears and answers our prayer.

Remember, God can handle your doubt, your anger, your fear, your grief, your confusion, your raw feelings and your questions. He really can.

The BP Oil Crisis. The Gulf of Mexico. 35 miles away. 4 a.m. The BP staging area. Twice a week a group of clean-up workers, men and women, huddled together as I led them in prayer.

"Why do you come to pray with us," asked a weary fishermen turned clean-up worker?

"I come because there is a God and He hears and answers prayer."

"I'm about to lose my boat," says he. "Would you pray for me." I held his hand and did just that – we prayed. As our prayer time ended I gave him a "black rock" – "This is to remind you that someone is praying for you. Remember, there is a God and He hears and answers our prayer."

Twenty... minutes later my cell phone rang.

"You don't know me and I don't know you,' said a woman. "I live in California and I just watched a news report about the plight of the poor fishermen. God told me to payoff the balance on a fishermen's boat. Can you help me with that?"

"Yes. I can. He and I just prayed at the BP staging area."

Eleven days later I handed a $13,000+ check to an astounded fishermen and his wife. Then I gave her a "black rock."

"Know this," says I to the fishermen and his wife. "There is a God and He hears and answers prayer."

When your feelings are raw, when faith seems weak, here's a faith builder: Wherever you find yourself, whether it's at the top of the mountain or in the depths of the deepest valley, God is there, and because He cares for you, you can live courageously, even if you don't like the way the ball bounces.

When your heart is troubled, when faith seems weak, remember, God can handle your doubt, anger, fear, grief, confusion, and your questions. He really can.

Several contemporary writers, building on the works of Augustine of Hippo, Thomas Aquinas and others, have reduced the relationship between the intellect (thinking) and emotions (feelings) to an equation. The equation describes a big "I" (intellect) over a little "e" (emotion).

In the normal affairs of every day living the big "I" is over the little "e" with intellect, informed by emotion, guiding us through life's routine (I/e). When we encounter adversity, or distress, or stressful events or experiences, the big "I" and the little "e" will swap places (e/I). This flipping process is normal.

As the event or experience is assessed and processed, eventually the big "I" will resume its natural position, being informed by but not dominated by or guided by emotions, the little "e".

If, however, after a reasonable passage of time the little "e" is still in the position of dominance, psychological impairment, emotional disturbance and spiritual distress will follow.

Unresolved grief is one of several types of situations that can cause this type of regress. Most of us know someone who is bogged down, fixated and unable to advance in life because of the long arm of the past.

The spiritual approach, in my estimation, is to have a different equation. I would suggest an "F" over a big "I" over a little "e" – Faith over Intellect over emotion. A popular hymn reveals why – "Faith is the Victory" – not feelings. (Remember the caboose?)

A man holds up a cardboard sign: WILL WORK FOR FOOD. You see them everywhere; people begging for money with signs reading 'Homeless,' 'Out of work Vet,' or 'Will work for food.' But what are the stories behind the cardboard signs. Here's one.

"I saw you sitting here and the Lord led me to pull over," says I.

Strange how God works, isn't it? Strange.

"Do you have a church home, a church family, a pastor?" I asked.

"Boy, I must look terrible," says he – and he did. He looked more like a human skeleton than a man. His clothes were grimy. His hair was matted. He was a mess, simply a mess.

"Brother John, its me (and then he said his name). I was shocked.

I hadn't seen him since pre-Katrina....and, now here he was, in such terrible shape, so terrible that I did not recognize him – a beggar and a pan handler, begging for food, holding his sign.

An ancient proverb says "first the man takes the drink, then the drink takes the man." His alcoholism had taken him alright, it had taken him where he never thought he would be – homeless, hopeless, a beggar and a pan handler on the rough streets of the city of New Orleans.

We talked awhile – about life, about his predicament, about the old days, about Christ and His wonder working power – and we prayed, oh, how we prayed.

"There is a way out of this," I shared, "there is a way through. If I never see you again, if you forget everything I've said, remember this – even now, God still has a wonderful plan for you and for your life. As an old hymn says, "It is

WHEN I CAN'T FIND GOD

no secret what God can do; what He's done for others He'll do for you."

As we parted I gave him a "black rock" and promised him a miracle. My wife says I always promise people miracles. Well, I'm guilty. I promised him a miracle – and, God gave him that miracle. He was in church the following Sunday -- got his acts together, landed an out-of-state job – what more can be said?

When your feelings are raw, when faith seems weak, remember, there is a God and He hears and answers prayer. And remember, God can handle your doubt, anger, fear, grief, confusion, and your questions. He really can.

Here's another faith builder.

He was a pig farmer; and he was drunk...shouting obscenities, cussing and waving a pistol every which way as he stepped into my church office.

"I'm gonna blow his blanky-blank head off," he shouted as loudly as he could. "I'm gonna blow his blanky-blank head off, I tell you...blow his blanky-blank head off."

Somehow (by the grace of God) I was able to calm him down. His story? His son had gotten him drunk and had the ole pig farmer sign the title deed to the pig farm over to the son. Then, the son , after filing the necessary papers, promptly had the ole man evicted.

"I'm gonna blow his blanky-blank head off," shouted he to the top of his lungs. "I'm gonna blow his blanky-blank head off, I tell you...blow his blanky-blank head off."

He agreed to wait a day and allow me the opportunity to talk with the son. I did and had no success, none whatsoever. The son was as hard as nails.

Then, the next day came....

"I'm gonna blow his blanky-blank head off," shouted he to the top of his lungs. "I'm gonna blow his blanky-blank head off, I tell you...blow his blanky-blank head off."

His old pick-up truck kicked dust and gravel everywhere as he left the church parking lot. I called the sheriff's office as a precaution. About twenty minutes later, with lights flashing and sirens blaring, an ambulance passed by followed by a police car headed in the same direction as the ole pig farmer.

"Oh. No. Dear God. He's killed his son."

But, he hadn't. About ½ a mile down the highway he had flipped his pickup. The back wheel was still spinning when I got there.

He had a stroke." said the emergency room doctor. When I saw him the next day his face was contorted. His arm shriveled, bent and twisted with his hand near his chin. He couldn't see, He couldn't speak.

"He probably can't hear, either," said the doctor.

Day after day for nearly two weeks I whispered God's plan of salvation in his ear, always closing the prayer by saying, "Ask Jesus to come to you, and He will. Talk to Jesus in your head. Ask Jesus to come into your heart. Talk to

DR JOHN DEE JEFFRIES

Him in your head. Ask him to come to you – He will come."

One day I was completely caught off guard and startled. As I finished praying over him the ole pig farmer's arm suddenly reached toward me. Grabbing my neck he pulled my head toward his face. With a raspy voice he said, "Jesus came to me! Jesus came to me! Go tell my son about Jesus. Tell my son I love him and God loves him too."

Two days later he died.

Let me say it again: when your feelings are raw, when faith seems weak, remember, there is a God and He hears and answers prayer. And remember, God can handle your doubt, your anger, your fear, your grief, your confusion, your raw feelings and your questions. He really can.

For many, feelings are often contradictory. Is it that way for you? Sometimes, feelings encourage faith. Sometimes feelings contradict faith. Genuine biblical faith focuses on Christ – nor on feelings. Remember, the locomotive, coal car and caboose?   Fact – Faith -- Feelings

Chapter 8
Faith and Fear

"Fear strengthens Faith. God supplies faith to enable us to overcome our fears. He supplies grace to enable us to walk through life's most difficult valleys. Know this: God has appointed a time, a place and a circumstance for faith to ultimately triumph over fear. When that time comes you will see that God has used every event and experience of fear to strengthen your faith – to enable you to Advance through Adversity."   -- John Dee Jeffries, The Last Martyr

Khaki-Colored Uniforms. Brown Shoes. Brown Belts. And, oh yeah -- And Little Purple Clip-On Ties. School Uniforms. I wore one; so did all of the other boys.

As I shared earlier, I was raised in a very religious home. My parents were faithful in their religious obligations in raising their children. Because of their faithfulness, I received a strong religious education in both elementary and high school.

Like the other boys and girls in our school, I attended church every school day. Sometimes, I felt pushed...even so, I was always faithful in my attendance at church and tried to be a "good boy" as best as I was able.

A "good boy"? As best as I was able? Sometimes, I guess its safe to admit it now, sometimes I wasn't very "able" – or at least that's the way it seemed. Memory, you know, shapes and colors our understanding and interpretation of such things.

Memory? Thinking about 2nd grade. I was in the school yard, decked out in my Khaki-colored school uniform. I wasn't very "able" and I wasn't being "a good boy." I was teasing and taunting another boy – when – in the heat of battle I reached toward him, grabbed, then yanked his clip-on purple tie – then I threw it as high in the sky as I could. And, what to my dismay, the tie went up, up, up, then on the way down, it landed on the other side of the school yard fence in the backyard of a neighboring house.

"I'm going tell teacher," the boy shouted. "I'm going tell teacher."

Thump. Thump. Thump. My heart raced. Fear. Anxiety. Guilt. Shame. Fear. Anxiety. Guilt. Shame.

Quick as a whip I climbed over the old New Orleans style wooden fence to retrieve the kid's tie. (I say "New Orleans style wooden fence because there is a distinction. This wooden fence was made of long 16" board that ran sideways, with each board running 12' – 16' feet – and stained with a blue, red, brown and purple stain.)

Just as I located the kid's purple tie two of the biggest, loudest barking, meanest looking dogs I'd ever seen appeared out of nowhere – growling and chasing after me. They had the biggest set of glistening dog teeth I'd ever seen. Quick as a lick I jumped as high as I could and climbed back over the fence – and threw the kid's purple tie as far away from me as I could across the school yard.

"Did you take this boy's tie, Johnny? Did you take his tie."

The moment of decision had come. All of my religious education was suddenly on trial. All of the spiritual investments that had been made – by my teachers, by my mom, by my dad – this was the moment of decision.

"Did you take this boy's tie, Johnny? Did you take his tie."

"NOPE," says I, as I put on my best 'I'm innocent face.'

"NOPE."

The first line of old English poetry I encountered in college had a line that in substance said, "Of all the gifts God gives us, Oh. That we might see ourselves as others see us."

What the teacher and everyone else saw that day was a little boy whose school uniform was completely smeared with blue, read, brown and purple stain.

"Look at your hands, Johnny. Look at your hands."

They were purple – stained with purple.

Thump. Thump. Thump. My heart raced. Fear. Anxiety. Guilt. Shame. Fear. Anxiety. Guilt. Shame.

Fear. I was caught purple handed. Guilt. Over what I had done. I told a lie. Shame. Over what I had become. A liar.

And, the greatest tragedy of all – everyone knew. The other kids. Teacher. Principal. Mom. Dad. AND, GOD. Yipes.

The Bible says, "….be sure your sin will find you out." – Numbers 32:23

Fast forward twenty-three years. I'm no longer a child – but I have some – three children to be exact.

"Daddy. Daddy. Come quickly. They're breaking the back yard."

Behind the shouts and excited voices of my children I could hear the sound of machinery – in the back yard. My children were city kids and my wife and I were city folk – living on the outer edge of a small town in rural Mississippi. (Our first pastorate).

"Every year we plow up this here field for the preacher and his family so they can have a vegetable garden. You know, fresh vegetables, canning food and all that."

He and some of the men of the church plowed the "back yard" (city word for "field") three or four times that week. The following Saturday they dropped by and gave us seeds, all kinds of seeds, to be sown in the new, soon-to-be "preacher" garden.

"A foot apart and two inches deep," says he. And we did just that. The children pulled out their trusty school rulers and measured depth and distance, depth and distance, over and over again. (It was a horrible first time experience for this city boy – and the city boy's children weren't jumping up and down about the depth and distance, depth and distance thing either.)

It really didn't take too, too long to do the depth and distance thing (yipes.). Suddenly, crops were coming up, everywhere. It also really didn't take too, too long, I might add, for the weeds to start coming up too, everywhere, and I mean everywhere -- and I mean everywhere, and I mean everywhere (you get the picture -- I mean the weeds kept a coming, and the weeds kept a coming........ a coming, and a coming, and a coming, and)

I think the word on the street was that the preacher's garden "got away from 'em, yes sir, the preacher's garden done got away from him. City boy, ya know."

Seemed everybody knew that the preacher's garden "got away from 'em" but – me – the preacher and the preacher's family. I knew we had an ugly garden overrun with weeds, but, goodness you should have seen the size of the okra, and the giant bell peppers, and the squash – especially the squash. Our squash was so big and large – they looked like a giant flying saucers. We thought for sure that we would win some kind of award or something....but, I'm getting carried away and you probably already know that we didn't win any award, no sir, not a one. We didn't know it then but the vegetables should have been harvested when they were smaller, much smaller. God intended it that way. (City Folks)

But, we did gain the attention of some black birds. Bunches of 'em would line up on the telephone wires that passed through and above our garden. The black birds seemed to be conversing, one with another, you know, talking things over. As if on signal they would swoop down into the corn patch (which grew "perfect" corn on the cob).

If we talked too, too loud or made loud noises they would fly back to the safety of their telephone wires -- and wait -- and talk some more while they waited. Then, whenever we went into the house they would stop their talking and swoop down again into the corn patch. They were having a jolly time – at our expense. Nothing else was edible – but the corn sure was.

We solved that problem, yes sir, we did and right quickly too. We may have had the ugliest garden in the county but we had the best looking scarecrow ever.

When the black birds saw that scarecrow you could almost hear 'em talking: "Who in the world is that scary looking guy?"

"He looks mean," I think I heard one black bird say, "and we better not go into that garden any more." And, they didn't – which brings me to the issue of fear and the Devil's scarecrow.

In the garden were blessings for the black birds – a field of delicious corn – but, they allowed a harmless, helpless scarecrow keep them from that blessing.

I reckon (that's a country word, reckon) I reckon that the Devil's got his scarecrows too. Know this, "God has not given us a spirit of fear." And, you probably already know who has – the Devil and his scarecrows.

What is it that keeps you awake at night, worrying? The Devil and one of his scarecrows. As long as he can create that fear – well, step beyond that fear – there just might be a patch of blessing beyond it – just for you.

If you don't remember anything else from this chapter, remember this -- fear is not from God but from the devil. (2 Timothy 1:7)

Take inventory – a check-up from the neck up – and make a "Fear List." What are you afraid of? Are you hindered because of fear? Some common fears are fear of death, loneliness, people, authority, commitment, heights, lack, germs, closed-in spaces, flying, dogs, cats, failure, rejection, being laughed at, and even fear of fear. The fear list seems to be endless.

If you're afraid of something and want to overcome that fear, you'll have to face your fear and not run away from it.

When we were children we were often afraid of the dark, the boogeyman under the bed, the monster that hid in the closet and the dentist. Eventually we learned that boogey men and monsters don't exist and the dentist knows what he's doing. We outgrow fears, but we never seem to outgrow fearing. Its this spirit of fear that hinders our experience of God. We can be so preoccupied by our fears that lose sight of God and His presence with us.

Here's a fact that makes this more challenging. When Adam and Eve disobeyed God they encountered fear. In Genesis 3 we read that "the LORD God called unto Adam, and said unto him, Where art thou? And he said, I heard thy voice in the garden, and I was afraid..."

From that moment till this the ethic of this world is fear. This world operates on an underlying premise of fear. Run a stop sigh and you're instinctively looking in your rearview mirror. Do something wrong, violate a principle, commit an offence and fear suddenly appears. Tell a lie, big or small – you'll find fear lurking in the shadows. Fear. Fear. Fear. That's the whole ethic, the underlying premise, the modus operandi of this world's system. We have been raised in a fear environment. Consequently, when things go wrong, or when we do wrong, the first emotion that rises up within us is fear.

Fear has many dimensions. Someone once said that depression is "fear turned inward." Feelings of despair and depression are different kinds of manifestations of fear. So too is anger.

It happens so often that it seems natural. We actually become comfortable with fear. We're afraid that we're not going to be able to succeed in life. Or, we fear that we won't be able to tough it out as we encounter adversity. We fear that we can't handle this, whatever the this might be. This test is too challenging. It's one test too many. This trial is going to be a little bit more than I can bear.

Remember this: the ethic of this world is fear. The ethic of God's Kingdom is love.

Two men came to my office. One was operating out of the ethic of this world -fear. The other operated out of the Kingdom of God – love. The first man was desperate, fearful and afraid – wishing that he had never been born. The irony of the situation is that the second man was battling a similar set of circumstances; but, this second man, rather than operating out of fear, operated out of love. The second man, rather than entertain fear walked in faith. Rather that "turn inward" he reached outward. Rather than walk in fear, he walked in love. God's love chases fear away. There is no fear in love. But perfect love drives out fear (1 John 4:18). God hath not given us the spirit of fear; but of power, and of love, and of a sound mind (2 Timothy 1:7).

A spirit of fear. It's more common than you might realize. Benjamin. His name was Benjamin. He was a teddy bear, big, good-natured, always smiling, the kind of guy who made peole relax.

His story was one of tragedy – and fear. His first wife died in a single car accident several years before we met. In the aftermath, just before we became friends, Benjamin married his second wife. She was a lovely person, recently widowed. She and Benjamin were happily married. Both seemed to have a greater appreciation for marriage through the loss of their prior spouses.

One day Benjamin was doing some mechanical repairs on my vehicle. After the job was completed I headed back home. When I arrived home the telephone was ringing. It was Benjamin.

"Come back! Come back! She's dead!"

When I arrived back at Benjamin's place he was in the middle of the road in front of his house, on his knees with his hands raised to heaven.

"Why God? Why? Why God? Why?"

His wife was dead. Heart attack.

Several months later I became pastor of First Baptist Church, Chalmette. Benjamin and I maintained, then eventually lost contact.

About two years after the death of his second wife I heard that Benjamin was living with a woman, cohabitation. This wasn't the Benjamin that I knew. Though the woman very much wanted to marry, Benjamin refused. We did some long distance counseling. We talked. We prayed. Benjamin was adamant – "No marriage."

Somehow, through the death of his first two wives Benjamin had become convinced that he was under a curse – any woman that he married would die. The Devil's Scarecrow. Benjamin and his companion never did marry.

Benjamin had a spirit of fear.

One final thing about fear and the distance it creates between us and God. When sin came into the world Adam and Eve immediately covered themselves and hid from God. The reason? Adam gave a simple answer: "I was afraid" (Genesis 3:10).

Chapter 9
Faith and Fear (Of Death)

"We talked about death. The husband and I, we talked about it. We did. I always thought," says she, "I always thought about our death in a sort of romantic kind of way. I thought that when death came for one of us, well, the one that died first would sort of pass 'gently into the night.' But, when he died, well, there was nothing 'gentle' about it....and, there was nothing romantic about it either. His death was hard. Long. Drawn out. Messy. And...."

Thinking about our conversation led me to think about a time when I was not yet a man, yet, I was no longer a child. It was one of those strange times when I thought I knew it all. I was driving dad's car through City Park in New Orleans with Genny, my future wife, seated in the passenger seat. As I recall we were somewhere near the City Park golf course.

Its seared in my memory -- the golfer taking a swing at his ball – when suddenly, into my line of sight between the golfer and me came a man putting a gun to his head – and pulling the trigger.

As the golfer dropped his club to run toward the afflicted man, I pulled the car to the side of the road and ran to see if I could help.

From a few feet away, the dying man looked like a fallen tree. His body was facedown. He was dead less than a minute. The golfer and I stood there looking at him. There was a sudden twitching, a quiver in the dead flesh of the man as he lay there.

"He's alive. He's alive. My God, he's still alive," said the golfer. Shock ran through me as the dying man's head turned toward us. His small closed eyes suddenly opened. He slowly raised his head, then just as slowly turned and looked at us – then his head fell back to the ground and he died.

When he died, well, there was nothing 'gentle' about it....and, there was nothing romantic about it either. His death was hard, not long and drawn out, but quick. Messy. And....

My stomach churned. The golfer threw up.

Those eyes. Those sad, sorrowful eyes. Many things pass from memory, dissolve, dissipate, disappear – but not those eyes.

There's another set of eyes that are etched into my memory – not the eyes of a man, but of a woman. As her eyes looked into mine, she said words that I'll never forget.

Sad and lonely she sat on the front pew of a church, crying with her hand using a white handkerchief to wipe away her tears then cover her face.

The year? 1995. It was not a good year for this pastor. It was one of the saddest years in all of ministry for me.

A minister friend, young, at the height of his music ministry – collapsed and died while running through an airport to catch a flight for an oversees mission trip.

A few months later a long time member of one of our mission churches, a backbone in the mission work, was tragically killed in an automobile accident. Her loss was a devastating.

No. It wasn't a good year.

A member of my ministerial staff – one of my best friends – on Christmas day.... And automobile accident... His wife was killed... A daughter was barely alive, clinging to life by life support.... Another daughter was permanently paralyzed from the waist down... And my best friend – a broken neck – and a broken heart.

During the same time-span a long-term pastor friend died. (he and another pastor friend actually recommended me to the Pastor Search Committee of FBC-Chalmette)

No. It wasn't a good year.

During this same year – 1995 – two teenaged boys, members of another of our mission churches, were killed while riding on a bicycle – a hit-an-run driver. Hundred's of mourners passed through our mission church offering condolences to the mothers.

Sad and lonely she sat on the front pew of a church, crying with her hand using a white handkerchief to wipe away her tears, then cover her face.

And now I was down on one knee, seeing that face – and looking into those sad, sorrowful eyes. Those eyes.

Many things pass from memory – but not her eyes. And as her eyes looked into mine, she said something I'll never forget.

"Oh. Pastor John. Oh. Pastor John.
God can do anything – except make a mistake."

Two thousand years ago Jesus attended a funeral – the funeral of a friend. He spoke. Before He spoke, however, He did something. "Jesus wept," says the fisherman, John, who attended the funeral and wrote down what Jesus said and what Jesus did. "Jesus wept."

Jesus was not powerless nor was He helpless when He encountered death that day – yet, He wept. Jesus wept because death had intruded into a family

WHEN I CAN'T FIND GOD

– and snatched someone loved from that family.

Listen. Death has never been, is not now, nor will it ever be something that brings joy to God. Open your Bible and you encounter God as He is – He is the God of Life. He speaks and this place is teeming with life. He speaks and hearts begin to 'thump' Life-giving blood begins to coarse through veins and lungs begin to breath. Because God is the God of Life.

Then, sin came into the world and with it a dark companion – death. Sin is like an inherited disease – a terminal disease – and we all have it. It is passed from generation to generation. We all sin. We all die.

God hated death so much that He "gave His only begotten Son [so] that whosoever believeth on Him should not perish but have everlasting life."

Death may be sensationalized in our culture. It may be glamorized in the movies. We may even carry romantic images about our own death and the death of people love dearly. Death is not our friend. I repeat – Death is not our friend. Death is a foe.

And, Jesus said, "I have overcome...." No sting. No victory. Only life everlasting through Christ. Christ has delivered His children from the fear of death – and we no longer need to live in bondage to that fear (Hebrews 2:14-15).

"Come, please. Please come. Come before night."

His voice was frantic, filled with fright – fearful. He and his wife had attended but not joined our church years earlier, and, now – they were in a thick of trouble.

"I don't know if she's insane or on the verge of insanity – something's wrong. Come, please. Please come. Come before night."

Later – mid-afternoon – I went to their home. I saw her before she saw me. I was at the bottom of a curved stairwell as she carefully and cautiously started down. She had aged since I'd last seen her – about five months earlier.

She was startled when she first saw me. Instinctively, she drew a quick, deep breath and just as quickly drew her hand to her chest. Then – her eyes – her eyes revealed that she was dealing with a greater fear.

"What are you looking for," says I?

"He's not here yet," says she. "He usually comes at night. But, you never know. He may come tonight. You never know."

She spoke hesitantly about her fears, about her anxieties and about a little graveyard next to a now abandoned white clapboard church.

"I must get out of here, while it is day. I must, I must have air."

Centuries ago, Christians sometimes celebrated a believer's death as his "birthday" – their day of entry into heaven. They celebrated because they believed what the Bible had to say about death, i.e., Christ has delivered His children from the fear of death – and we no longer need to live in bondage to that fear. They understood (and believed) that "death had no sting and the grave had no victory." (1 Corinthian 15:55).

A broken moon spilled through two large oaks in front of their home. A flush of pink and red azaleas danced as gentle twisting winds blew. It was later that night. I had returned, as promised. She was on her couch, which was strategically placed so that she could see both the front and back first floor entrances to her home. She had somehow come to believe that when the Angel of Death came – he would come through either the front or back entrance. She had so positioned herself that if he came in the front, she would escape through the back; and vice versa.

She disbelieved Scripture – disregarded its sufficiency – and rejected all attempts to help her. I lost touch with them and never heard from them in the aftermath of hurricane Katrina.

What about you? What about me? Can we conquer our fear of death? Everyone must eventually battle fear. Some fear heights. Others fear flying. Still others fear drowning, or snakes, or mice. Many fear death. Some call the fear of death a primal fear. No one is immune from death. The fear of death, however, afflicts everyone. In some situations fear of death can actually paralyze us – grip and hold us -- such as the lady who feared the Angel of Death.

Can we conquer our fear of death? It depends on who the "we" is referred to in this question.

If you are numbered with the unsaved, the lost and you are not born again -- you should fear death. As written in Hebrews 10:31, "It is a fearful thing to fall into the hands of the living God."

If you are numbered with the saved, the redeemed and you are born again – you have nothing to fear. David understood that he had nothing to fear when he wrote, "Even though I walk through the valley of the shadow of death, I will fear no evil, for you are with me." (Psalm 23:4) Paul understood this too. He writes to young Timothy (and to you – and to me). He wants us to know that "...God has not given us a spirit of fear..."

Paul could sleep peacefully, night or day, with the thought that the Angel of Death could come for him at any time... And you can sleep peacefully too. And so can I. And so can that lady – through faith in and assurance from Christ. He is our peace.

Thanatophobia, or fear of death, is a rather complicated phobia. Most people are afraid of dying. Some fear being dead, while others fear the actual act of dying. If fear affects your day-to-day affairs then you might have thanatophobia.

Morbid, obsessive feelings and fears about death are, for many people, rooted in religious beliefs. These feelings and fears are more powerful and intense when a person is experiencing religious uncertainty. These obsessive fears often lead those afflicted to withdraw from God – thereby intensifying that sense of the absence of God.

When a person approaches the time of their death or the death of a loved one, frightful feelings and fears may also surface.

11:30 p.m. "Can you come?" says the voice on the other end of the phone. "He won't make it through the night." Thirty minutes later we met in the front room of her home. A hospital bed filled the room. On it was a man, her husband. Tubes, wires, and machines were everywhere.

"He's not saved," says she. "And he's going to die tonight."

"One other thing," says she. He's completely paralyzed. He can't talk or move – he can't even squeeze your hand or finger."

I bent over the hospital bed and began sharing Christ, slowly whispering God's plan of salvation into his ear. I closed my share time with him by leading him in that special prayer of faith and repentance. Trusting in the grace and generosity of God I urged him to invite Christ into what remained of his life.

"Do you think he invited Christ into his life," says she.

"I'm going to try to find out," says me.

"Mister, I know you can't talk and I know you can't even squeeze my hand, but I noticed while we were praying that your lip quivered and moved, just a tad. Sir, if you invited Christ into your life – if you can, would you smile..."

Unbelievably, he flashed one of the biggest, sweetest smiles I think I'd ever seen. Before sunrise, he died. I call him the man who smiled his way into heaven.

Sometimes, things seem hopeless. Sometimes, it seems as if all is lost. The key word is "seems" – what "seems" to be is not always what is. The world of appearances is often deceptive. So, be patient. Trust God..... and smile.

Let me share about another man, a man who through faith in Christ overcame the fear of death.

The odds were slanted against him – and he knew it. The cards had been dealt – he held a losing hand. There was a time when Jesus said, "This sickness is not unto death." (John 11:4)

"No, sir – Jesus may have said that about that fella' back then, but what I have is gonna' kill me. It will, yes sir, it will, and I have no qualms with that – this sickness – my sickness -- IS unto death. What I have is gonna' kill me."

Courage. Conviction. Character. Mr. Whitney had that and more, much more. He had Christ. But, He was alone. Alone in the world. No family. No real friends – just a handful of acquaintances. Once married – now divorced. No children. Alone. All alone.– and, well, as I looked at him then and as I think of him now, well, that was sad.

A poet (I believe it was Robert Frost) once noted that man is ultimately alone when he is sick; but, he is no more alone than "when he dies alone" -- and this man, Mr. Whitney, was sick – and alone – and dying.

"I didn't choose this battle, no sir – it chose me."

DR JOHN DEE JEFFRIES

Like the apostle Paul when his "time of departure was near." (2 Timothy 4:6) Mr. Whitney had made a declaration of surrender – to Christ, many years earlier – and now, more recently as the time of his departure – his death -- approached. He had lain down his arms, shed his armor -- the battle would soon be over.

Sometimes a message from the dying can give pause to the living. I was Mr. Whitney's final farewell. I think we both knew that. His words became few, then gradually diminished.

Courage. Conviction. Character. Christ. Without words Mr. Whitney spoke. These were his final message. I held his hand. The hushed voices of nurses continued as they listened....

"Little – Less – Nothing," wrote the poet, "Then that ended it."

Then that ended it?
Did it?

Do we live our lives for what will last
Or for what will fade away?
Are we striving for the world's praise
Or for Christ's "well done" one day?
-- Author Unknown

Chapter 10
Faith and Foolishness

Faith Like Potatoes, is a true-to-life movie based on the life of a Angus Buchan, a South African farmer. In the midst of a devastating drought, Buchan receives a word from God -- plant potatoes.

He's ridiculed, mocked and heckled, much like the biblical Noah when he built the ark. Even his pastor attempts to discourage him from planting potatoes. At a critical juncture in the movie the pastor says, "Angus, There's a fine line between faith and foolishness." Then he tells Angus that if he really believes that God told him to plant potatoes then he should plant potatoes.

"There's a fine line between faith and foolishness."

In the Bible there are many instances where faith appeared to be foolishness. Noah is a prime example. So too is Abraham's faith decision to move to a place, "not knowing whither he was going" (Hebrews 11:8).

In Faith Like Potatoes Angus shares with his wife that God has called him to be foolish for Christ, and every seemingly ridiculous choice he makes from that point forward yields a miracle that glorifies God.

"There's a fine line between faith and foolishness."

Remember – a fine line. Don't confuse faith with foolishness. If you do, you'll get tripped up and God will appear distant.

During WW2 some Americans were stationed on a small island in the South Pacific. Monkey meat was a real delicacy on this island. The islanders showed the Americans how they captured monkeys.

1. Put an apple in a narrow-mouth jar
2. Tie a rope around the jaw
3. Tie the other end of the rope around a tree
4. Wait patiently

Eventually a monkey will come along, look curiously in the jar, see the apple, reach in and grab it. The monkey's hand easily compressed to fit into the jar but his fist, holding the apple, was too large to pull out. The monkey, however, would predictably refuse to let go of the apple. The monkey was, in effect, tied to the tree by the rope, the jar and the apple. And very soon – monkey stew.

Now think about this for a moment. Was the monkey too stubborn or too stupid to let go of the apple? You know what? It really doesn't matter. The result was the same – one dead monkey.

Now for the real question: Did the monkey have the apple or did the apple have the monkey?

There are many things that bind us. As long as we foolishly hold on to them, their power over us continues. It is only by letting go that we become free. So, what's making a monkey (a fool) out of you?

Os Guinness, a prolific Christian author, in the concluding remarks of his book, The Gravedigger File, discussed 'The Three Fools And The Devil's Mousetrap."

The first fool, according to Guinness, is the fool proper. He is a fool because he is worldly-minded. As such he lives his life foolishly, focusing on things below (the temporal) rather than on things above (the eternal).

The second fool, says Guinness, is the fool bearer. The fool bearer is opposite the fool proper. The fool proper mocks and ridicules the fool bearer and those things that are not of the world. The fool bearer endures, is resilient, because he is a "fool for Christ. Consequently, "the fool (fool proper) hath said in his heart, 'There is no God'" (Psalm 14:1) and regards the things of God (and the things of the fool proper) as foolishness.

The third kind of fool is the fool maker. He builds up expectations in one direction then throws everything into reverse. God is the ultimate fool maker – constantly making a fool out of the Devil.

The Devil's Mousetrap, by the way, was the cross of Christ. God, the ultimate Fool Maker – set the trap.

Satan, did not fully understand that the cross was his defeat and therefore facilitated our Lord going to the cross. Satan set the events in motion which insured his defeat and destruction.

God, the ultimate Fool Maker set that trap and made a fool out of the Devil. Trrraaaapp

The Devil, however, is highly skilled and very adept at fool making too. Think about this.

I know little if anything about medicine. But I saw something the other day on TV – about medicine. What I saw made me sit up, then sit back, and say, "WOW. That'll preach." (And, it did.)

But, before I tell you what I saw on TV let me tell you about Deacon Bill. Deacon Bill was a fine young deacon, young as far as most deacons go (30ish)

WHEN I CAN'T FIND GOD

and "fine," that is, until that ole Devil convinced Deacon Bill that our youth minister was a scoundrel, a genuine scoundrel – and ought to be tarred and feathered and run out of town on a rail car.

"Why, he misuses the church bus, doesn't dress right, combs his hair crooked, plays his guitar too loud – why – he even stole money from the church -- I'm telling you he stole money from the church."

Now everyone knew that was a pack of foolishness. Everybody. But, that last charge -- "stealing money from the church" – well, that kind of charge, from a deacon of all people, well, somebody had to check that out and clear things up – and somebody did – in fact, a bunch of somebody's did. But even though wiser heads than mine (about a dozen or so with calculators) even though they checked things out and even though all concluded that there was no wrong doing, none whatsoever – that young ole deacon cried loudly, louder and louder. He just absolutely, totally, believed that the youth man was a genuine scoundrel, a scoundrel who had stolen from the church.

"That's a lie from the Devil," said the Chairman of Deacons to that young ole deacon. "That a lie from the Devil. That ole Devil is the Father of Lies and you are believing the lies of the Devil."

Which brings me back to that TV program, you know, that TV program about medicine.

The discussion was about placebos. Placebos are really not medicine, nope, and they're not real pills either. They're actually little white sugar pills that look like medicine – but they're not medicine and they're not real pills – not a one of 'em.

Now, according to that TV program, experiments were conducted that proved that a certain percentage of people, when given a placebo, are cured of their ailment – because they believe the sugar pill is real medicine. But, it's not. (In essence, they believe that something – a sugar pill – is something that it is not – real medicine.)

Now, get this, they actually believe it so much they their ailments are cured. Physical changes actually occur because they believe. Body temperatures drop. Cholesterol is lowered. Blood pressure and Blood sugar levels too. Imagine that. Physical changes actually occur – because they believe. (There's a lesson about faith in there, I believe, for an enterprising preacher.)

Oh, but wait, there's more. The man on the medical show said that when they took that little sugar pill and coated it like a real pill and colored the pill "red" – the percentage of people cured increased. WOW. What's that all about?

Not finished yet. They also found that if the placebo was placed into a capsule with one end colored 'yellow' and the other end colored 'blue' – the percentage of people healed went even higher. And, hold on here, they further discovered that if the sugar was dissolved and put into a syringe with a needle – and injected -- an even higher percentage of people were healed.

Which brings me back to that young ole deacon, you know the one I'm talking about.

If a fella in a white coat, suit and tie can devise a strategy to convince folks that something that is one thing is something else, something totally different – well, what do you think the Devil, that ole Father of Lies, what do you think he can do?

That young ole deacon was had. What happened to him? Spiritual Placebo. That's right. The Devils got a whole bottle of 'em too. That ole Devil gave some to that young ole deacon and that deacon got sick – spiritually sick – and began doing the Devil's work. He did. You see, the Bible says that the Devil is the "accuser of the brethren" – not us. That's the Devil's job – That wasn't that deacons job – not your job – not my job. (Don't get me wrong. We're not to turn a blind eye to bad stuff in God's church. Not at all. But, there are people who handle stuff like that in God's church. Godly people who know how to do whatever needs to be done – without harm.)

Spiritual Placebos. Seems to me that there's a whole lot of 'em going around these days – watch out.

Oh. About that deacon -- He left our church. Went to another one. Then left that one. Then went to another one. Then left that church too. (You get the picture.) Spiritual Placebo! That ole Devil made a monkey out of him and mingled faith with foolishness – and that, in and of itself, is foolishness.

And that youth man? Why he's not young anymore and he's not a youth man any longer. That fella' grew a little older and is now the pastor of one of the finest, largest, most respected Southern Baptist churches in a prominent Alabama college town. We're proud of him too.

Like the monkey you can grab a hold of foolishness. Or like that young ole deacon foolishness can grab a hold of you.

Many have lost that twinkle of the eye and that sparkle of a smile. They are the casualties in the battle – victimized, duped and deceived by one of the enemies most effective weapons – foolishness and deception – spiritual placebos.

When this kind of defeat occurs you will battle with skepticism, cynicism, lustful thoughts, unbelief and doubt, and more, more, more – much more. Passivity will surface and spiritual lethargy and inertia will begin to dominate – and your awareness of and your sensitivity to God and His presence will become distorted. Know this: the very nature of deception is that the deceived are not aware that they are deceived.

Sometimes the presence of God doesn't look like the presence of God. In Matthew 14:24, the disciples failed to recognize Jesus as He came to them walking on the water.

Following the death, burial and resurrection of Christ two dejected dis-

WHEN I CAN'T FIND GOD

ciples walked a lonely road to Emmaus (Luke 24:13ff). The resurrected Jesus was walking with them – step for step -- but they didn't recognize Him; but, Jesus was there, with them.

Mary Magdalene didn't recognize Jesus immediately outside the tomb until he called her by name (Jn 20:14ff). Jesus was there, with her.

Like the early disciples we sometimes find ourselves needing to be open and receptive to this fact -- Sometimes the presence of God doesn't look like the presence of God; but, Jesus is there, walking with us. Jesus is always with us.

My home air conditioning unit was broken. I didn't know the repairman and he didn't know me – and he definitely didn't know I was a pastor. He talked and talked and talked as he turned wrenches in an effort to repair my broken unit. Not too far away, high above the tree line, was a steeple on a church.

I remember quite well how troubled I was about our church at that time. There was inner turmoil, tension. Suddenly, this man made an observation about God's church. It was an insightful statement, one that immediately got my attention. It was as if this man was reading my mind. Here he was turning wrenches, a man, a simple man, a secular man -- not involved in anyone's church, making a singular statement about God's church. Immediately after he said what he said, his conversation turned back to trivial matters.

I had a choice to make: was I going to be open and recognize that God was present to me through this secular man? Or, would I spurn the presence of God and the possibility that He was speaking to me through this man.

Some would say, "That's foolishness." I would counter with sometimes the presence of God doesn't look like the presence of God. The key in these situations is biblical revelation and spiritual discernment. Without God's revelation and biblical discernment we run the risk of embracing foolishness. In essence, the Devil would then be making a fool out of us.

So, sometimes the presence of God doesn't look like the presence of God. In fact, oftentimes things in and of themselves are not as they appear.

Two little boys, imagine them if you will, two little boys with brown paper grocery bags cautiously tip-toe through an old, decaying New Orleans cemetery. It was one of the historic above ground cemeteries – and it was crumbling!

He who writes these things knows what he is talking about – I was one of those boys! Thaddeus was the other. Our mission? To gather as many empty locust shells as possible!

"Rumor has it that Tulane University is payin' as much as twenty-five cents a piece for them locust shells," boasted Glen Stokes. Glen was a neighbor boy who lived in a New Orleans camel-back, shot-gun house across the street from where I lived. Glen was older then me and Thaddeus – so he ought to know, sure enough, Glen ought to know.

Now, me and my friend Thaddeus, we knew where there was a ton of locust shells – the ole Lafayette Cemetery No. 1 on Washington Avenue, right across the street from the famous Commander's Palace restaurant. The cemetery is home to almost 500 wall vaults and for some reason known only to God, not man – locust seemed to shed their shells there.

For nearly four hours Thaddeus and I were like pirates gathering and hoarding our loot – empty locust shells! Now, its hard to imagine just how heavy a bag of empty locust shells would be. I can tell you, from experience, they weigh a whole lot more than anyone could imagine! Just thought I'd let you know that if you ever set out to gather some locust shells!

There's a few other things I think you ought to know, I mean, just in case:

(1) Cemeteries can be pretty scary places! To make matters worst, the above ground cemetery vaults in this particular cemetery were crumbling -- in a state of disrepair and decay. Looters and grave-robbers had broken into some of the vaults and graves! Some graves were even open! We saw bones – real people bones! For the very first time, Thaddeus and I saw a human skull! (Yipes!) Remember, cemeteries can be pretty scary places!

(2) It wasn't easy, no it wasn't easy, to gather thirteen brown paper grocery bags of empty locust shells. It wasn't easy; but we did it! Thaddeus and I – we did it!

(3) Painful Lesson #1 – Bigger boys – like Glen Stokes – sometimes play pranks on smaller boys! We were had! Glen Stokes – you are a liar! Liar, Liar, Pants on Fire! Tulane knew nothing about empty locust shells. He who writes these things knows what he is talking about!

(4) Painful Lesson #2 -- Sometimes, I think of the right thing to say – too late! Sometimes, I don't think at all!

(5) Oftentimes things in and of themselves are not as they appear. If we fail to discern biblically the Devil seizes that opportunity and becomes a Fool Maker – and we miss the presence of God

There were three of us, yes sir, there were three. Little Boys. We were good boys too. Why, we even had "merit badges" to prove it. And we were taught to avoid foolishness and always "Be Prepared."

Yes sir, there were three of us. We were part of a larger group of boys, just like us.... Little boys, good boys....put us all together and we were a Troop – a

Boy Scout Troop. And, all of us were on one of those special trips in the great wilderness called St. Tammany parish in south Louisiana, just above the town of Covington, to be exact – near the Village of Folsom.

We three, did I tell you, we were good boys, well, yes, of course we were, we were good boys because Boy Scouts are always good and always live by that special motto – "Be Prepared."

Well, we three were in the thick of the wilderness, away from the troop, working our way through the forest. We were surrounded by tall pine trees – and no telling what else. Lions? Bears? Tigers? Indians? The Loch Ness Monster? Bigfoot? Who knows what lurked in those woods?

Well, one of us, certainly not me, came up with a bright idea – we need to be prepared – so, let's cut down this tall pine tree then, after it falls, we can be prepared and make our own secret hideout. Good idea. We all agreed. To this day it surprises me when I recall how quickly three good little boys chopped down that pine tree. I mean the tree was at least thirty-forty or perhaps fifty feet tall.

Before you know it --- faloom – down came the tree – with a loud, loud roar – faloom.. Scared the heart out of us. Now, I don't know what was hiding in those woods, but we three good boys started running every which way as loud angry voices were getting closer and closer to us – and to the fallen tree. It might have been an Indian, or an angry farmer with a pitchfork, I didn't know who or what it was. I was just too, too busy running, running, running, as fast as I could to get away from that tree.

Later that night, around the camp fire, the troop leader told stories about trees, tall trees, and forests, thick forests and he told us about private property too – and about how little boys with axes could be dangerous, even to tall trees in the forests. (Even Smoky the Bear was concerned about trees and forests, says he.)

Then, he told everyone about THE tree. Every one was silent as he told about THE tree. Sweat was rolling down my face, my neck and my back. (Momma once said she had an eye in the back of her head – she didn't say that troop leaders had eyes back there too.) And then, he called all three of us good little boys before the troop, I mean the whole troop. And, I wondered, as I stood there sweating, sweating, and sweating some more -- how did he know?

The Bible says, "Be sure your sin will find you out" (Numbers 32:23).

Foolishness. I'm a fool for Christ – and that's not foolishness! Whose fool are you?

Chapter 11
Faith and Flesh

Back when I made my decision to receive Christ, four other men walked the church aisle as well. James and I became pastors. Al and another fine Christian, also named John, eventually became deacons. However, one of the five, Mack, didn't continue in the faith.

Unfortunately, through distance and the passage of time, I've lost track of Mack. I have, however, wondered about him often. I've prayed for him often.

You see, for some reason Mack simply didn't persevere. Perhaps he was like Demas (1 Tm.4:10) and loved the world more than he loved Christ. Or perhaps, like one of the seeds in the parable of the sower, he lacked something necessary to perseverance (Matt.13:18-22).

I imagine if you look carefully you can find a 'Mack' or two in your past too. They once stood tall for Christ but now, well, they're no where to be found.

Nearly twenty-five years ago when I began my pastoral ministry at First Baptist Church, Chalmette, a church leader shared his concerns with me about people who fall away.

"When I first got saved," says he, "I was given a copy of a workbook called 'The Survival Kit' for new believers. When I read that title, I thought to myself –I might not survive."

I wonder about him too. Like Mack, he is no where to be found.

I read a magazine article in a Christian magazine a number of years ago. The title of the article – "Saved By Christ – Lost To The Church."

While you think about these things, be careful. Make sure you're not a Mack. Be careful, you just might not survive.

There's a pull, an almost constant tug of the flesh. The flesh, like an octopus, has many tentacles, tentacles that reach for and touch just about every area of life.

........"I Ain't Goin' To That There 'Free Jack' Church."

WHEN I CAN'T FIND GOD

That's what he said. That's exactly what he said. "I Ain't Goin' To That There 'Free Jack' Church. I Ain't Goin'"

"Oh. We're a Southern Baptist church," says I. "We're Southern Baptist."

As he walked away he turned and shouted one final time, "I Said I Ain't Goin' To That There 'Free Jack' Church. I Ain't Goin' I said. I Ain't Goin'"

The little church where I served as pastor at that time was located in a rural community on the outer edge of the Village of Folsom in southern Louisiana. The little church was filled with good, hard-working, God-fearing, salt-of-the-earth people. They loved God. They loved one another and they loved the community that God had entrusted to their care. (And, yes, they even loved this man who rejected them so vehemently.)

During our ministry in Folsom we lived, loved and shared Christ with our neighbors -- and we helped one another meet the challenges of life. The people in that little "Free Jack" church shared down-home hospitality and genuine Christian love with everyone, with anyone. We had a powerful evangelistic ministry through that church during our tenure in Folsom.

That congregation was indeed a warm, loving, nurturing, deeply spiritual church family – but they were, according to the angry man, a "Free Jack" church – and that posed a problem for that man and for others like him. Originally, I thought that "Free Jack" was some new-fangled denomination that I didn't know anything about; but, it wasn't. It was a direct reference to a particular church – the church where I served as pastor in Folsom – the "Free Jack" church.

Here's the "Free Jack" deal: Each Sunday, on one side of the church, sat the Davis family. The Davis family members were fair skinned, blue-eyed, with straight light brown to blondish hair. On the other side of the church sat another branch of the same Davis family. The members of this branch of the Davis family were dark skinned, brown-eyed, with dark brown to black curly hair. Mingled within both branches of the Davis family were people of various shades and colors. Most of them were related.

Just about everyone, however, had their family branch rooted in the same family tree -- with each branch passing through an infamous Mr. Davis, a prominent plantation/slave owner who lived several generations earlier. Hmmm.

What can be said about this. Simply this: Our world is a world of differences. There are political differences, philosophical differences, ethnic differences – you name it – our world is a world of differences. These differences translate into divisions that sometimes cause hatred, anger, strife and more.

In Christ, all our differences are nullified. We become the one body of Christ. Our differences are put to death. While the world may fight over their differences, while society may argue over their differences, and our communities may be divided because of differences -- the church is a place where unity and peace should prevail. But, the flesh, with its carnal tentacles, reaches there too.

Remember the children's song? Red and Yellow, Black and White, they are precious in God's sight. Jesus loves the little children of the world (and He loves His big kids too.)

Throughout history there have been those who have been destined for greatness – but didn't make it. The culprit? Quite often it's the flesh. By the way, if you want a simple definition of the word "flesh" – just write the word backward and draw a line through the letter "h" – wow.

A friend, Sam was one of those gifted guys who didn't make it. Sam was definitely chosen and called by God – a genuinely gifted leader – a man destined for greatness. Everybody knew that. Everybody was sure about that. Yes, sir, Sam was a man destined for greatness – but he didn't make it.

One thing stood in Sam's way – Dee. Yes, sir, her name was Dee. Sam was enamored with Dee, smitten, head over heels in love with Dee, or so he thought. Dee, however, was a dangerous woman – and Sam knew it – but he was willing to risk everything for Dee – even his call by God to greatness.

You see, Dee was a devilish women, a dangerous kind of woman, a conniver who had attempted, several times, to trick Sam out of money -- and more. She kept trying, too, over and over again. And, Sam? He just kept coming back for more and more. Eventually, Dee turned Sam against his family, his church family and, in a more than sinister way she tricked and turned him away from God.

Even though Sam hated what was happening he refused to end the relationship. I wish I could share that Sam's story had a good ending, but, instead of ending the wicked relationship Sam allowed himself to be enticed further and further away from his family and God. He fell deeper and deeper under her spell and deeper and deeper into sin.

It wasn't until he was put into prison that he saw the severity of his mistakes and the error of his ways. In that dark, dank prison Sam, like the prodigal son, finally "came to himself." He realized that he had by his own choice "seared his conscience" and that he had by his own choice become numb to what Dee was actually doing to him. He was bewitched, enticed, in bondage – under her spell – and in prison.

Even though Sam was destined for greatness, he learned the hard way that his powers, his abilities and his strength were gifts from God – gifts that WERE NOT unconditional.

When we're in bondage we excel at minimizing our enslavement. We think just a little longer, just one more time and then I'll quit, then I'll stop, then I'll turn away– then everything will be all right. But, that's a lie perpetrated in the pit of hell. What is true is that as we move deeper and deeper into dominance by the flesh -- the "one more time" becomes a life-dominating sin.

Ask my friend Sam (Samson) about that. (His story is told in the Bible book called Judges, chapter 16). Through his unsavory involvement with Dee (Delilah) he learned the hard way that even though a man is destined for greatness, well, Sam(son) Didn't Make It. The flesh. Another tentacle.

Her name was, well, that really doesn't matter. She could be your wife, your sister, the gal in the next office – she could be you. (And, I might add, this is not a "female only" issue, but for this venue I'll address it as such.)

She was basically a "young" believer, in her late forties and saved for less than two years. She was one of the sweetest, happiest people I'd ever met. She loved God, loved God's church and loved her pastor. She had the ability to wiggle her way into your heart, and she did that often, and with many people, both inside and outside the church. Her joy and happiness were contagious, conspicuous and continuous. Everybody was happy when she was around. She carried sunshine wherever she went, wherever she was.

Then one day.....

Yep. There's always that one day, isn't there?

Then one day..... she came into my office wearing a really "sad sack" kind of face. Nothing fake about what I was seeing either – she was too distant and too distracted and too disturbed mentally and emotionally to fake this dour, sour kind of mood.

"What's up with you," says I. "Nothing." But, we both knew better. "Sit down, take a load off your mind," says I. "I've never seen you this way -- so depressed, so down. So tell me, what's up? Empty your bucket, tell me about it."

"Well," says she, after a long pause. "I've been reading this book and it says if 'this' happened to you when you were a child, then this is what will be happening to you when you're an adult."

What followed was the painful story of a wounded woman, a story I've heard often, more often than any could imagine. Sitting in the shadows of our congregations, and, yes, sometimes standing at the forefront, are wounded women who bear a silent secret of the 'this' that happened to them– sexual abuse.

After she talked for awhile I assured her that God's Truth could and would "set her free." – and it did – three days later.

"So you've been reading this book for four days now," says I, "and you find that what the book is saying is true in your life – you're experiencing these things, negative things, and you're depressed, really depressed about that – down in the dumps."

"Yes," says she. "Yes, I am really, really very depressed about what I have been reading and about what is now happening with me."

"Were you depressed last week before you read the book?"

"No," says she, but I didn't KNOW about these things before I read the book."

"No," says I, "let's correct that -- you didn't BELIEVE these things until you read the book. There's a difference."

She tilted her head and raised one brow, not knowing what to say or what to think. "Well," says she as the other brow raised, "what do you mean?"

"I mean that before you read this book you were one of the sweetest, happiest people I'd ever met. You were like that because you were reading and believing what the Word of God says about you. God said, 'You were a new creation; old things had passed away and all things – everything about you – was new and fresh.' -- and that made you happy and joyful."

She tilted her head and raised one brow a second time.

"God said that you were 'born again' and you were and you experienced a newness of life – and that made you happy and joyful. You believed what you read about yourself in God's Word and that made you happy and joyful – and you actually became a new person altogether."

She tilted her head yet again then inched closer as I continued to speak.

"Now, you're reading and believing this other book, a book that describes your old life and the end product of that old life, negative things, and you're depressed, really depressed about that. What that book is talking about is real. These things do bind many, many women to a painful past. God's Book, the Bible, talks about something that is real too, something very real – and it shows how you can be set free from that painful past."

The corners of both eyes began to moisten. She reached into her pocket, retrieved a tissue, then wiped the tears away.

"Choose now, but choose carefully, and choose wisely. Which book do you believe, I mean, really believe? Who do you believe-- God or the person who wrote this book? What do you believe, what do you really believe about yourself? God says you've been severed from the power of the past and the power of that old life, and a new power, the very power of God has been unleashed and now flows within you and through you. You've been set free."

Her prescription, with respect to her past and her past experience: "Go home and give yourself a pity party from three days. On the third day, the day of resurrection, believe, know and trust "the power of His resurrection" and thank Him for that power. You have been – not will be – but have already been set free."

Final note: God seldom removes painful memories, but He can and does heal them as we bring them to Him. Another tentacle of the flesh, severed.

God can and does heal.

No matter how, no matter when and no matter where the flesh touches yo, it always creates wounds, woundedness and brokenness.

"Turn your wounds into wisdom," said an anonymous poet. "Most things break, including hearts," added another.

WHEN I CAN'T FIND GOD

In "Harry Potter and the Order of the Phoenix" J. K Rowling writes – "Some wounds run too deep for the healing." On the opposite end of the spectrum is the old adage "Time heals all wounds."

Just about everyone has an opinion, a thought, an idea – about woundedness, brokenness – and healing. And therein lies the fly in the ointment. Some falsely believe that "some wounds run too deep" – and cannot be healed. While others mistakenly put faith in the passage of time to heal.

Know this. Time heals nothing. Only Christ, only Christ, truly heals. Know this. There is no wound so deep, so hidden, that Christ cannot reach it – and heal it.

Her eyes. Her eyes revealed an anguish, an inner anguish that she could not hide. Though it beat in her chest, her heart was a dead heart. Yes, her heart was dead -- Dead to life. Dead to love. Dead to God. Tortured by her past. Tortured by her secrets. Tortured. Tortured. Tortured. Her wounds, her woundedness, her scar tissue – were real, terribly real – and she desperately needed healing.

I looked into her eyes.

"I see your scars."

"They're part of my past," says she.

"Perhaps," says I, "but know this, scars are only present where wounds have been healed."

Chapter 12
Faith and Fantasy

I once heard of a bishop who was greatly troubled by the lack of success of the church and the clergyman of his day. In desperation he approached a famous actor and inquired of him concerning the matter. The actor replied: "We actors speak of imaginary things as if they were real. Yet, many clergymen speak of real things as if they were imaginary."

Let it be known that this pastor/author has great esteem for and a high view of Scripture. Let it also be stated emphatically, with conviction, that the Word of God deals, not with imaginary things, nor with figments of human imagination, but with truth... Holy truth that is wholly true... "truth without any mixture of error."

I would also interject at this point that truth never needs a defense. When Christ was on trial before Pilate He was silent. He offered no defense because truth is not to be defended – truth is to be believed.

"God said it! I believe it! That settles it!" is inscribed on a bumper sticker. "No," related a preacher from yesteryear. "God said it and that settles it – whether you believe it or not!" And all the Bible-believing people of God said: "Amen!" Why? Because truth is to be believed.

The Scripture speaks very clearly of a very real "adversary" – "a roaring lion" – a very real, not imaginary – personality called the "Devil." The great majority of the people of God, however, in the normal day-to-day living of life, live as if the Devil didn't exist. Many live as if the Devil was not real, as if he were imaginary, as if he were a figment of the imagination of unenlightened past generations – pure fantasy.

Several years ago Hal Lindsay wrote a book entitled "Satan Is alive And Well On Planet Earth." Tragically, though the church has been and is engaged in a relentless war without frontiers, the adversary has become an invisible, melting kind of enemy who has successfully created an everywhere yet nowhere feeling in the midst of the struggle. On one hand we have a crowd finding demons and devils under every rock and bush, always casting out something, somewhere, everywhere. On the other hand we have a crowd relating the reality of the Devil to the misguided, collective religious consciousness of our unenlightened historic past.

Dear friend, hear me. The Devil is alive and well, and further, not only is he alive and well, but he and his kingdom of darkness are very active and very aggressively working and weaving their darkness into our lives, our families, our communities and into our culture. One of his primary devices? – fantasy!

The Bible tells us that "faith is the substance of things hoped for, the evidence of things unseen" (Hebrews 11:1)

Sometimes the things of faith come from the inside (the substance of things hoped for), sometimes from the outside (the evidence of things unseen).

Through our internal and external experiences we color our understanding of faith; we color our understanding of faith with language. Sometimes, unfortunately, our language is more fanciful than factual.

Faith, in its simplest form, is the meat and potatoes of the Christian life, the coin and currency of the Kingdom. "Without faith it is impossible to please God" (Hebrews 11:6).

Some people think that if they really believe the truth it will open the door to fanciful experiences with God and the supernatural.

Because the Bible utilizes images biblical faith is easily linked to fantasy. Also, because the Bible utilizes propositional truth biblical faith is easily linked to facts.

"Propositional truth," says Josiah Lewis, author of The Sketchbook of Scarlet, "is great for people who idolize having the right answers, because if you express yourself in logical propositions it's easier to assess your rightness."

In essence, the propositional nature of biblical faith provides explanations. Faith, however, is greater than propositional explanations. Faith is experienced. It is experiential.

Roughly one half of the Bible deals with experiences that people had as they lived lives of faith. Therein, however, is the fly in the ointment – our modern day proclivity toward fantasy. The proliferation of literature and movies that focus on angels, demons, territorial spirits, spiritual warfare and more have given birth to many erroneous ideas that are inconsistent with the teachings of the Bible. The biographies and narratives of people's lives in the Bible communicates truth, not only as a explanatory message, but as an experience.

Frank Peretti's books, real page-turners, will have you burning the midnight oil. The Present Truth and Piercing The Darkness, written by Peretti, are two classic novels of the Christian thriller genre. In both of these books

Perettii draws on the dualistic structure of the universe – there is a physical universe and there is a spiritual universe. One is temporal. The other is eternal. Peretti, using the language and imagery of fantasy, tears back the veil that separates these two realities. He illustrates the linkage between the two in a way that is consisten with the biblical revelation.

Late one night many years ago I listened intently to a very colorful interview that a Christian radio host had with Peretti. The interview was enlightening and entertaininng and filled with conversation that honed in on deep and profound truth. In the midst of their conversation Peretti told several personal stories relative to faith and fantasy.

The first evidently happened when Frank was a young man, new to the faith and filled with a passion for God and the things of God. During that phase of his Christian life Frank shared that he had a proclivity that was slanted more to the fantasy side of faith rather than its factual side. He wanted more than explanations concerning Who God is – he wanted to experience God deeply, personally, experientially.

In substance Frank related that somehow he became strongly convinced that God had called him to be the replacement for Billy Graham. His conviction was so strong, his faith so passionate that he persuaded his father to drive him to Billy Graham's headquarters to talk about how he and Graham would handle the transition of the ministry.

Peretti, the great story teller, related how he and his father drove half-way across the country to the headquarters of the Billy Graham Evangelistic Association in Manitoba, Canada. He recalled walking back to his father's car, confused, baffled, puzzled and embarassed.

"You mean you didn't call first and make an appoiintment with Mr. Graham."

"I thought that since God let me know I was to go then surely He would let Mr. Graham know I was coming!"

Frank recalled his answer to his fathers question. In substance he said, "No. I didn't call Billy Graham. I thogted that if God revealed this to me He surely would have revealed it to Billy Graham."

In the interview, Peretti then shared some of the lesson he had learned concerning faith, fantasy, imagination and other dynamic aspects of faith and spiritual discernment. He closed the interview by sharing another situation he had many years later.

Peretti shared that after the conclusion of a speaking engagement he was approached by a mother who was distraught and deeply concerned about the spiritual condition of her son. The son, much like Frank in his younger years, had a proclivity that was slanted more to the fantasy side of faith rather than its factual side.

She shared that her son, who believed that he could walk on water, actu-

WHEN I CAN'T FIND GOD

ally walked off the deep end of a pier to demonstrate his faith in his ability to do this.

"He nearly drowned," related the hysterical mother.

"Have you or your husband ever had to drive your son to Manitoba, Canada," asked Peretti.

Peretti then told the mother that she ought to thank God that it didn't cost her or her husband the time and expense of a trip to Manitoba, Canada, for her son to learn a valuable lesson about discerning the difference between faith and fantasy.

Sometimes, when we're in the thick of trouble – when faith is stretched – we began to fantasize, not about walking on water, but about how or what God is going to do to help us. If we're in financial trouble, we began to fantasize about how God is going to use some unknown rich uncle, or a wealthy person, to help us. Or, we falsely think that God is going to have us win the lottery. These illusionary fantasy's provide a false sense of peace and a temporary relief. We form false presumptions and begin to fantasize about what God will do – then when the rich uncle doesn't materialize, or we don't win the lottery – our faith constricts, making God seem more distant, aloof and uncaring.

"Now faith," says the writer of the Bible book called Hebrews, "faith is the substance of things hoped for, the evidence of things not seen" (Hebrews 11:1). This is an excellent definition of faith. Faith is substance. "Sub" refers to "that which is below." "Stance" refers to "that upon which we stand."

We stand on faith, a faith that is substantive in its structure. Faith is not a fanciful wisp of cloudy miraculous spiritual dust. No! Faith is substance. Faith is beneath us, upholding us.

Faith is also evidentiary in nature. Faith is evidence. Evidence is that which can be validated. Genuine biblical faith is validated. Evidence is that which can be verified. Genuine biblical faith is verifiable. As we stand on the Word of God and act on it (regardless of how we feel), God promises a good result. He does not promise a rich uncle, or produce a winning lottery ticket. He does promise a good result.

Faith is the firm belief that somehow God will work "all things together for good" (Romans 8:28). We may not see how God will do this and we may not know when – but we have the confidence and calm assurance that God will provide a good result.

This is not pie-in-the-sky. As we continue to walk with God we discover that our growing faith sustains us through hard times. It gives us confidence to take the risks we need to take to continue to learn, grow and mature.

Faith based on the evidence of things not seen is one thing. Fantasies concocted to avoid responsibility are totally different.

Faith mingled with fantasy isn't based on evidence, seen or unseen. Its based on imaginative fabrications – fanciful thinking. The focus when we stand on fantasy is not on God and the good result that He promises. The focus is on whether or not God will work things out exactly like I want God to work them out. Convenient fantasies may distract us and provide temporary relief, but that relief will only be temporary. They also cause us to avoid dealing with reality, delay our accepting responsibility and lead us to dodge rather than resolve unpleasant circumstances.

In the aftermath of hurricane Katrina God gave me an assurance, an inward sense of certitude, that our church would be rebuilt. All seven of the church buildings that formed our pre-Katrina campus were destroyed. I had no congregation. There was no community. The entire population of St. Bernard parish, where our church was located had been displaced. I was living eighty-five miles away. Yet, I was convinced that the church would be rebuilt debt-free, without the traditional financial support of a congregation.

Someone once asked me while in the midst of the Katrina recovery crisis, "how are things looking?" My response, "well, with the eye of the flesh, not too good; but, with the eye of faith, things couldn't be better! God said that 'goodness and mercy shall follow me all the days of my life.' So, with that promise, with the eye of faith, things couldn't be better."

"Is this Dr. Jeffries from Chalmette, Louisiana" she asked.

"Yes, but I'm living in Livingston. Louisiana, at the moment -- displaced by the hurricane, you know," says I. She was a church secretary from a Baptist church I'd never heard of in Beaumont, Texas.

"Is that close to Baton Rouge or Port Sulfur?"

"Pretty much, somewhat," says I. She went on to explain that her pastor, whom I did not know, wanted to meet and treat me to breakfast the next morning.

So, there I was at the Waffle House in Port Sulfur, Louisiana, early the next morning when he walked in, a giant of a man, a Texan. I mean, he was the biggest pastor I think I've ever seen. The man must have been at least six foot eight, perhaps even taller. He was a Big Preacher, a Big Texan with a Big Heart serving a Big God.

"Read an article about you and the pastor's in St. Bernard parish meeting, praying and struggling after the hurricane. Man, the Holy Spirit jumped all over me and for some strange reason my heart broke for you, John, my heart broke for you. Tell me your story," says he, "I read that you were still pastor of the church from eighty-five miles away. Tell me your story."

We talked, ate breakfast, drank coffee and made connections. Along the way we discovered and discussed many things, things about God, things about our churches, things about ourselves and things about relationships. His dad, it seems, unbeknownst to either of us, was one of my long-ago seminary professors.

WHEN I CAN'T FIND GOD

He put one of his big hands on my shoulder and prayed one of the sweetest, most encouraging prayers – the Holy Spirit jumped all over me.

Just before he drove away he blew the horn and rolled down the window of his car. "This is for your church," says he. "Remember, God will always supply your need." And with that he drove away.

Sometimes, when the going gets rough I think about that unknown Texas pastor and the unknown congregation he represented.

"Remember, God will always supply your need."

That's not foolishness – that's fact.

And, inside the envelop? Well, later that day I made a deposit into the new building fund -- $25,000.00 from a pastor I didn't know from a church I'd never heard of...

"Remember, God will always supply your need."

That's fact – not fantasy.

"I'm stuck," says she; and stuck she was. Two failed marriages, a string of broken relationships, a stint in a rehab plus a long history of missteps and misdeeds. She was stuck, alright, very much so – stuck in anger, stuck in fear, stuck in despair. Every time she tried to move forward in life, the long arm of the past held her back. Stuck.

"I can't go on," said she. "I just can't."

That was a long time ago. Today, everything is different. She's a radically-changed woman. She's moved on in life – moved forward – one step at a time. How's that? Her first feeble step was to receive Christ.

"Repentance and faith," said I. And, she did just that – she turned from Something (her Sin) and turned to Someone (her Savior) – Christ. She invited and received Christ into her life. She turned her will and her life over to Jesus. Then, she took a second step, then a third, then many additional steps were taken – and she took them, one step at a time. Each step was a step of faith – rooted in faith, not fantasy.

An ancient Chinese proverb says that "a journey of a thousand miles begins with the first step." She took that first step, that first day, many years ago. With the dawn of each new day she took yet another step forward, then another, each day traveling a little further and a little deeper into the new life given by Christ.

Stuck? Not any more.

Running. Running. Running. Always in a hurry – yet getting nowhere. Nowhere. Nowhere. Nowhere. You're......

S-T-U-C-K. S-T-U-C-K. S-T-U-C-K.

Ever feel as if you're running as fast as you can – just to stay in place? It's madness. Madness. Madness. It's the old Sisyphean effort. But, if you stop running – more madness. Sheer Madness. You're......

S-T-U-C-K. S-T-U-C-K. S-T-U-C-K.

"Being stuck. Who likes that? Few if any of us like being stuck. We want something new but struggle to let go of the old. We hold on to old ideas, old beliefs, old habits, even old thoughts and old thinking patterns. Sometimes we know we're stuck; sometimes we don't. In both cases we have to DO something." -- Rush Limbaugh

Do something? Here's several keys, several things to DO....

Stop FANTASIZING... Start TRUSTING...Trusting Christ.
Without Jesus you cannot do anything.
Only He can get you un-stuck.

She was once married to a crazy man. Her marriage, filled with drug and alcohol abuse and chaos, quickly came to an end – but not before the birth of her son. Her ex – the crazy man -- burned his brain out sniffing this, snorting that or shooting up. He lived on the streets, under houses, under bridges – just about anywhere – and she couldn't handle that – and she had a baby son to take care of.

"Life was hard back then," said she to me as she came forward while the church sang "Just As I Am." She related how she and her baby boy once lived in St.Tammany parish in a storage shed behind the Winn Dixie.

"Just until I got on my feet," said she. Her cousin was the store manager.

"Things were hard back then," said she, "but that was yesterday. Today things are better -- still hard – but better -- I have Jesus."

She talked a little longer then she looked intently at me.

"I have a prayer request," said she. "That's why I'm coming forward. But I don't want to tell you or anyone else what the prayer request is. If I did, you or someone in the church would probably take steps to answer my prayer. I want the answer to this prayer to be specifically and undeniably from God – without outside interference. It's nothing big, but, I want the answer to this prayer to definitely be from God."

Three weeks later at the close of the church service she came forward again to the front of the church carrying a brown paper bag. Her face was glowing. She wore a smile. She gave testimony of her "secret" prayer request and shared with us how God – and God alone – answered her prayer.

Then, with her now five-year-old son standing next to her she said, "Son, show the people what God gave you."

And he did. He reached down into the paper bag and out came a base-

WHEN I CAN'T FIND GOD

ball glove. He rolled his little fist into a knot and began popping it into the leather glove. I can still see her standing there with one hand raised to heaven – "Thank You, Jesus."

"Amen. Amen." shouted some folk. Others wept silently. Still others stood, applauding. And many wondered, "What kind of God is God-- Big Enough to create the Universe yet Close Enough, and Tender Enough, to give....

Complete the above sentence with your need and make it your "secret" prayer request. Count on God for a Good Result

Chapter 13
Faith and Facts

"It ain't gonna happen," says he. "I'm five million in the red and there's no way out. It ain't gonna happen."

The 1980s. That's when it happened. The American economy boomed then busted. No industry was harder hit then the housing industry; and, the man sitting across from my desk was upside down – in hock -- for five million dollars.

I was pastor of a small mission church at the time, simultaneously attending seminary, and also simultaneously working as a financial consultant for a firm in New Orleans.

If ever there was a man who owed a debt he could not pay – this was the man. We talked a lot, prayed a lot, and laid out a financial recovery plan. Slowly, very slowly, through a delicate process of buying, selling, financing and refinancing the debt began to diminish.

There was, however, another debt he could not pay – his sin debt. In the midst of our strategy meetings he eventually received Christ. He invited Jesus into his heart and turned his will and life over to Christ. He discovered the truth of the old hymn, "Jesus paid it all, all to Him I owe."

After several months we hit a brick wall. His financial indebtedness was down to less than five hundred thousand dollars. He had restored his good name but could not find any wiggle room to maneuver what remained of his financial debt. His financial house of cards collapsed; but, he did not.

That's a fact.

"Everyone experiences difficulties and I'm not exempt," said he. "If I've learned anything it is this -- Jesus of Nazareth, the Prince of Peace, gives unshakable peace and I've got that peace."

It was mid-summer, 2010. On Memorial Day, a team of evangelical St. Bernard parish pastors motored out onto Lake Borgne and prayed together over the BP polluted waters of the Gulf of Mexico. We also shared the Lord's

WHEN I CAN'T FIND GOD

Supper and asked God for relief. It was my privilege to be a part of this small faith group. Before we left we poured salt over the water, commemorating a biblical act of healing the waters by the prophet Elisha. It was a powerful spiritual experience for all of us. I am thankful that I was there sharing the special time with genuine brothers in Christ.

Several weeks later our churches worked together again to distribute food to BP afflicted fishermen and their families. For several hours a long line of vehicles stretched nearly a mile alongside the highway waiting to receive their food boxes. We shook hands, prayed with each carload of people and when it was over discovered that we had distributed food to 5000 people.

Some personal observations about feeding 5000 people. First, when we hit that special "5000" number, unlike Jesus, we had nothing left over. Nothing. Second, unlike Jesus, when we hit that special "5000" number, not only were we depleted of food, we were depleted of energy. We were worn out and exhausted. Lastly, even though we had nothing left over and even though we were exhausted we discovered that each of our congregations are truly unbelievable people accomplishing the impossible for the glory of God.

That's a fact.

A young fireman was electrocuted – a training accident – right in front of the firehouse. His teeth shattered. The ends of his toes were blow off. Several of us held a spoon in his mouth to keep him from swallowing his tongue while others tried to hold him down as his body twitched and bounced on the hard concrete drive.

Afterward, the man who was responsible for the accidental electrocution, another fireman, came to talk with me and my friend Joe. Joe was my first convert – and a very strong Christian.

"You Guys Know God. I Don't. Would you guys pray, please pray, that God will keep him alive? John, Joe, I'm scared to death. Please ask God for me. You Guys Know God. I Don't."

These were strange words, strange words from a man who had constantly teased and taunted Joe and me because of our Christian faith. But, then again, perhaps these words were not so strange after all. You see, when the chips are down, I mean, when they're really down and you have no where to turn – people instinctively seek God.

We did pray, Joe and I – and the young man miraculously survived....and, the taunting and teasing stopped. That's a fact.

There are many implications that could be drawn from this incident. I'll only focus on one: when your faith in Christ is visible, others may tease and taunt you; but, deep down, they know you have the real deal. The genuineness of your fait and its visibility, well, when the chips or down the fearful, the hurting, and yes, even the lost will draw strength and encouragement from you – and be nudged toward faith in Christ.

DR JOHN DEE JEFFRIES

However, if you hide your light under a bushel. Or, If your testimony is tarnished, or If your character is questionable – or, If you conduct is suspect – or, If your conversation is crude and vulgar – why would anyone come to you or want what you have. No one. That's a fact.

"You Guys Know God." said he, "I Don't."

1988. Our family was excited. Our son was gearing up for college. We had our short-list, our long-list, our things-to-do-list, our check-list and our lists of lists – do this, do that, don't forget the other. (I'm sure you've been there – done that.)

At some point we purchased a little Volkswagen beetle from my minister of youth for our son to go back and forth to college and to drive around campus.

My wife says I have a strange sense of humor – and sometimes, sometimes she might be right. Take this Volkswagen beetle, for instance. Since this would be our son's first venture away from home, on a whim I bolted a framed 5 X 7 black-and-white photograph of me to the dashboard of the vehicle. It was one of those strange, eerie photographs. No matter where you sat in the car, mye dull dark eyes on the photograph followed you. We humorously called it the Dashboard Dad.

"Remember, I've got my eye on you, Sean. I've got my eye on you."

"Yeah. Yeah. Yeah," says he, "but it bugs me dad – Dashboard Dad is always watching me. It's like surveillance."

Oh, one additional thing. I don't know how I did this but once the Dashboard Dad was bolted to the dashboard, well, we never could figure out how to get it off. The car was eventually passed on to our daughter for her college years – with Dashboard Dad's eyes still doing their thing.

"Remember, I've got my eye on you, Sheri. I've got my eye on you."

"Yeah. Yeah. Yeah," says she. "but it bugs me dad – Dashboard Dad is always watching me. It's like surveillance."

Surveillance? In Psalm 32 God, the Father, says to His children "I've got my eye on you." His eye is not on his children for surveillance but for a higher purpose – "With my eye upon you, I will counsel you" says the heavenly Father, and He adds "and I will instruct you and teach you in the way you should go."

Was my purpose surveillance? No. Hardly. The photo didn't and couldn't provide surveillance. My purpose was simple. A scene from the movie "It's a Wonderful Life" illustrates it best. A young George Bailey was in a tight situation. He didn't know what to do. Mr. Gower, the pharmacist was drunk, slapping young George around, and unknowingly demanding that George deliver a deadly drug to an unsuspecting client. Young George was in a panic. His head was spinning. He was getting light-headed. As everything around him was spinning, faster and faster, he suddenly saw a sign on the wall of the drug store. It simply said, "Ask Dad. He Knows." Implication: Sure, I was having fun with the kids – but I really had something else in mind – "If you get in a tight – call me."

If you're in a tight, you can call on the Heavenly Father – That's a fact.

An old hymn says it well, "His (the heavenly Father's) eye is on the sparrow, And I know He cares for me; His eye is on the sparrow, And I know He watches me"

The Father says to His children "I've got my eye on you." Surveillance? Naw. When you in a tight – "Ask Dad. He Knows." Call on Him! He will answer. That's a fact.

A greased pig, with his mouth tightly tied closed, can make some pretty terrible sounds. And, so too do little boys – who get too, too close to the greased pig. Take it from someone who knows. I've been there and done that.

I was a little boy (maybe ten, maybe eleven) and the greased pig with his mouth tied closed was running straight toward me – making a terrible racket – some of the most scary noises I'd ever heard.

The place? Clay Square in New Orleans. The event? The annual New Orleans Recreation Department playground fair. Plenty of candy. Plenty of games. Hot dogs. Hamburgers. Even a beauty pageant. My dad was usually the master of ceremonies for the beauty pageant.

The big attraction, at least for the boys and girls my age – was the greased pig contest. It was like the country had come to the big city – sort of. One thing about our greased pig was different, though – the large number of boys and girls (nearly a thousand, if seems) who were down right determined to catch the greased pig – well, they were all determined except for one little fella – me.

I wanted nothing to do with the greased pig. I was there for one reason and one reason only – to protect my reputation. There was no way I could stay home (even thought I didn't want to be there) goodness, a fella could be tarnished for life for doing such a thing as avoiding the greasy pig contest. The other kids would call you names like "chicken" or "yella belly" or even worse things. Besides, my dad, well, my dad.....

So there we were, at least a thousand or so kids in this massive circle of humanity -- inside of Clay Square. Out of nowhere a man emerges holding a squealing, greased pig. The pig smelled terrible. A gun shot drew immediate silent -- sorta like a sacred hush --then a loud roar of voices, kid voices. The greased pig contest was on.

"Look out," says a voice inside my head. My heart started thumping, and thumping, and thumping. That danged squealing greased pig was coming straight toward me. He was snortin' and a huffin' and a huffin' – his eyes were staring at me. I immediately started running the other way, faster and faster, away, away, – away from the pig, into a massive onrush of boys and girls coming from the other direction.

The rest of this story is hazy. As I ran against the flow of the crowd with the squealing pig and half a thousand kids hot on his tail, somebody's elbow hit me on side of the head. WOW. It hurt. Everything started spinning. I fell to the ground and grabbed a kids leg. I don't know who he was. I just held on for dear life. That kid squealed and squealed, squealed as loud as the greased pig. Wait a minute. The squeal wasn't a kid – it WAS the greased pig. What?

I was the hero. Somehow I had tackled the greased pig. Dad was proud, oh he was so proud. Dad even announced my name during the beauty pageant as the boy who caught the greased pig.

Lesson 1:
We live in a world of appearances. Things aren't always as they appear.

Lesson 2:
Some, who appear to be heroes, have hearts that "thump" with fear.

Lesson 3:
Life has a way of arranging circumstances so as to force us to face our fears. God is always there, especially when we face our fears. That's a fact.

Lesson 4:
(Write the lessons that you see in your Journal)

Chapter 14
Faith and Friends

"I loo-vee yoou, Bro-tho John," she whispered in my ear. "I loo-vee yoou, Bro-tho John," as she hugged me tightly, Sunday after Sunday.

I hold poignant, powerful memories of this very special woman She loved God. She loved God's church and she loved me, God's pastor. Through her love, her pure genuine love, I learned valuable lessons about the joy of hugging.

Every Sunday she gave me her secret "love letters" – but I couldn't read a word that she had written – not a word. She would write these "love letters" over a period of several hours every Saturday, then, when she and only she knew that the letters were complete, she would roll them together tightly and wrap a brown rubber band around them.

In our world, too often people with Down Syndrome are taken for granted and often overlooked by others. In reality, these special people are special gifts from God. They are some of God's greatest givers of love and of hugs. Someone once said, "If they ran the world, their ability to minister to others would not be wasted."

This special friend of mine is in heaven now. One day I'll see her again and we'll sit together and read those secret "love letters" – one by one.

In life, there are people who share our journey. There are also special people who not only share our journey but shape us in ways that are deep and profound. It seems to be woven into the fabric of life that we help and influence others and others in turn help and influence us. Our lives are largely constructed using bricks handed to us by others. Even the mortar that keeps everything together – given to us.

Which brings me to Nathaniel. Nathaniel (Faith and Formulas) is one of my six grandchildren. When Nathaniel was 3 yrs/4 yrs old he was securely seated in the back seat of my car – headed to Happy Paw Paw's house (Happy

Paw Paw – that's me).

"There's an airplane, Happy Paw Paw. There's an airplane over there).

"Where?"

"There, over there, Happy Paw Paw, over there."

I must have been looking the wrong way out of the wrong window. I didn't see the airplane.

"No, Happy Paw Paw, over there." (Nathaniel was getting frustrated with me.)

"Where?"

It became obvious that Nathaniel did not yet know the difference between right and left – so a fundamental life lesson began. Nothing profound. Nothing deep. But knowing the difference between right and left is an essential lesson that Nathaniel needed to learn and carry throughout life.

"This is my left hand, This is my right hand. This is my left ear. This is my right ear. This is the left window. This is the right window."

On and on we went – then came that miraculous moment – "Do you still see the airplane, Nathaniel? Where is the airplane, Nathaniel?"

"Its over there, Happy Paw Paw. It's on the left side. Look through the left window."

Mission Accomplished, sort of.

You know and I know that there were and still are many life lessons for Nathaniel to learn. He's a teenager now. (Another story) But, what about you? (And, what about me?)

In life, there are people who have shared and are sharing our journey; and, like everyone else there are some special people who have not only shared but have shaped us in ways that are deep and profound.

I doubt that Nathaniel remembers or realizes that Happy Paw Paw taught him the vital distinction between left and right. But, the shadow of Happy Paw Paw will always remain – hidden in the past as the one who shared a simple, yet essential life lesson that shaped Nathaniel.

Think for a moment. Who is back there, hidden in the past, perhaps unseen, standing in the shadows of your life? And, who is under the shadow of your life?

While learning the difference between left and right is essential– there are some bigger issues at play here. Things like "Rejoice" or "Regret" -- because of WHO or WHAT lingers in the shadows. The influence that lingers can either help or hinder our ability to experience the presence of God. That's a fact.

Alone. I conducted a funeral today – for a man I did not know. And, it appears, no one else knew him either. He was alone. Alone in the world. No family. No friends. Never married. Alone. All alone.

He was originally from St. Bernard. But, he bounced around the country – alone – and died in Florida. Poor. Broke. Alone. Two friends from long ago, a husband and wife, who lived in in Missouri heard about his death; and it broke their hearts to know that he was alone, all alone in the world.

The couple traveled to Florida, had the body shipped to St. Bernard. They covered the expenses of the funeral. They flew down to attend, and mourned and wept as they fully realized the plight of this long ago friend, a friend who was alone, all alone, in life and at the moment of his death.

Gilbert O'Sullivan once sang a song, in the 60's titled "Alone Again, Naturally" that focused on how easy it is for us to isolate and be alone. God said in His Word that this is not good: "It is not good for man to be alone."

In the movie "It's A Wonderful Life" there is a line that is spoken to George Bailey. He was in a crisis and felt alone, all alone. The line? "A man who has friends is never alone."

The best friend you can ever have is sitting in a Bible study class in a church near you. God has fixed things so that you never need to be alone. Hope to see you Sunday, in the church of God's choice.

A friend is waiting for you there, a friend who will nourish and strengthen you and your faith. That's a fact.

Conclusion

All of us have struggles that hinder our growth, diminish our passion, and hold us back. Several years ago I developed some special material to facilitate Christian growth among believers participating in a special class called "The New Creation Class." What follows is a small portion that was designed to facilitate spiritual growth. I call it the Passion Test.

(1) Make a few notes about the progress you've made as a Christian thus far. What are your high moments, thus far? What are your low moments?

(2) Be honest with yourself. What is it that's keeping you from being the person Christ wants you to be? And, what steps are you willing to take to become that person?

Remember, God is eager to help you, but, be honest, what's your next step? God wants you to know that you're not on your own – it's a cooperative effort.
There's a part that is God's that you cannot do (God has done His part and will do His part); and, there is a part that is yours that God will not do. You MUST do your part.
God assures us in His Word that you can be "confident of this very thing, that He which hath begun a good work in you will perform it until the day of Jesus Christ...(Philippians 1:6) [so] work out your own salvation with fear and trembling (Philippians 2:12). For it is God which worketh in you both to will and do of His great pleasure.
Think about it: In eternity past, before the world was created, God saw every person who would ever lie. He saw every generation, every period of history, every moment in time. He saw every circumstance and every situation tht would ever come into existence.
It's important for us to realize that nothing – nothing in your life or my life – nothing ever catches God by surprise. He sees what's coming, makes

provision both before and as it comes into existence, and interjects Himself into the situation and accomplishes His redemptive purpose – even in the midst of the most turbulent events, unpleasant situations and difficult times.

To illustrate, let's think about you. Science tells us that, like snowflakes, no two people are alike. Each person possesses a special uniqueness that makes them distinct from every other person. Implication: You're special. You – yes, you – you possess a special uniqueness. No one that ever lived before, no one that lives today and no one that lives tomorrow will ever think, feel, dream, walk or even talk exactly like you. No one else has your mind, your heart, your eyes, your ears, your hands, your mouth or your body.. You possess a special uniqueness that makes you distinct and different from everybody else. That uniqueness makes you who you are – someone special in the eyes of God.

And, God saw you, gifted with that special uniqueness that makes you who you are, even before the world was created, even before you had existence and He loved you.

Then God looked at all of the various countries in the world that would ever have existence and He loved them. He loved their uniqueness. He loved their people. God also looked at all the periods of human history and based on His love, He decided "when" an "where" you should live and have existence. (Acts 17:24-26, notice v. 26)

You see, God has a special purpose and a special plan for you and your life, based on His love for you, your uniqueness and the uniqueness of these times. And, through His love He has actually been negotiating circumstances to draw you to Him and to His special purpose and plan for your life.

Our goal in life – your goal and my goal – is not to decide what we want to do but to discover what He has purposed, planned and destined us to do. He did all of this so that you might seek Him – He can be found.

As we move to a close let me share something funny, yet amazing – something that is not too, too often seen.

Across from me standing in line at a local convenience store was a man and a woman, obviously a husband and a wife. Both wore matching tee shirts with coordinated writing on the front and back of their shirts. Behind the couple was man, a man with a big belly half hanging out and over his blue jeans. He too had a tee shirt with writing on the his shirt, but only on the front, with the writing stretched tightly from side to side.

Now I'm convinced that at least a couple of life messages can be found through these tee shirts. Just wondering. What do you think? Can you put together some life messages.

The first couple – the old guy, the husband, had a shirt that said "Old Grouch" and his wife wore a matching shirt that said "Old Grouch's Wife." The second guy, who really was out of shape wore a tee shirt that said "I Wish I'd Known I'd Be Here This Long – I'd Have Taken Better Care Of Myself"

Shirts that Talk. But What Are They Saying.

A memory, like a footpath, meanders backward as I remember and recall an earlier time. I was visiting someone who lived on a farm. Behind the house was an open field and woods. At a fork in the trail that ran behind the farm house was a big red barn and a barnyard – and horses, cows, goats, pigs, and chickens.

If I sit still long enough I can still hear the sounds, see the sights and smell the pungent smells. The ground was like mush, covered with barnyard animal tracks. What I remember most, however, was the sudden flush of dark storm clouds and the rush of activity by barnyard animals as they scurried to escape the sudden downpour.

As the rain fell, harder and harder, the farmer and I, like barnyard animals, ran for cover. Finding shelter near a chicken house we paused and what I saw next was, well, unforgettable.

As the rain continued to fall, in the middle of the barnyard a mother hen was cackling, louder and louder, calling her little chicks to shelter under her extended wings. The little chicks were racing and running for cover under the extended wings of the mother hen, escaping the rain, and the winds that swirled around them.

One little chick, however, did not heed the momma hen's call. It just stood there – alone, cold, shivering in the cold rain.

In the Bible and in life, Jesus likens himself to a mother hen, with wide, safe wings outstretched for protection and shelter in the time of storm or trouble.

In Luke's Gospel Jesus said, "how often I have longed to gather you as a hen gathers her chicks under her wings -- but you were not willing."

Hey. Is that you out there, troubled and blown about by the rough winds of life? Shivering? Alone? Sooooo Not Necessary.

God has plans for you and your life.

Through the prophet Jeremiah (29:11 MSG) God says, "I know what I'm doing. I have it all planned out--plans to take care of you, not abandon you, plans to give you the future you hope for."

You may think that God has nothing planed for you -- but He does. You may feel that God is busy working out His plans for others, but not you – stinkin' thinkin' – know this...

God has plans for you and your life.

And it's not just a hastily drawn up plan. It's a plan to give you a good and prosperous future – the kind of future you hope for.

No matter where you are in life, remember...

God has plans for you and your life.

A number of years ago my wife and I enjoyed an evening at a local restaurant. When the young waiter brought the check I felt led to write a little note on the receipt, a note just for him (I do that sometimes – when I feel led). The note was a simple note...

God has plans for you and your life.

Several weeks later my wife and I visited the same restaurant. The same young waiter eagerly shared how grateful he was for the note.

"I was down in the pits, feeling like a loser. I had just graduated from college, unable to find a job in my field – banking – I took this job serving tables. My mom has been praying for me. She was worried. I was worried. Everybody was worried. I was down in the pits, feeling like a loser....all those years of studying banking....

'Then I got your note. It was as if God was speaking – directly to me. I called my mom immediately and told her – 'Mom. God has plans for me and my life. God has plans for me and my life.'"

"How do you know," asked his mom?

"God sent me a note," says he.

A few weeks later we visited the same restaurant again.

"He quit," says the boss. "Got a job as a banker in the city."

I remember the young waiter shared he wanted to go into banking -- that was his major in college. God's plans were evidently unfolding.

About three years later my wife and visited a different restaurant.

"New Ownership" – read the sign in front of the building.

A familiar looking waiter came with the menu.

"You don't remember me. Years ago you left me a little note. God has plans for you and your life. I own this place."

Postlude

He was less than a year old -- and learning how to crawl. He would maneuver this way, then that. He was a genuine "rug rat" -- my son, my first born.

Learning to crawl is a key milestone in a baby's life. Crawling is a baby's first way of getting around by himself. It strengthens the muscles in preparation for walking. At about nine to ten months a baby will usually begin pushing off with his knees to get the boost needed to get mobile. And, goodness, my son was certainly mobile.

My wife and I were living in one of those old camel back, shotgun houses in New Orleans. The weather was turning cold and a big old match was taken from a large box of kitchen matches to light the open space gas heaters.

My son, our crawling toddler, a genuine explorer, was also very much attracted by the flickering flames of the open space heater. I was seated on the couch when suddenly my son bolted forward, crawling as fast as he could. He was totally fascinated by the colorful tongues of fire dancing inside of the open space heater.

Time was of essence as he rapidly raced and crawled on hands and knees toward the flickering tongues of fire.

"No. No. Stop. Stop. Quit. Quit. Burny. Burny."

My son immediately stopped dead in his tracks at the sound of my excited, raised voice. He looked, first at me, then at the little flames dancing inside of the space heater. And, he learned his first fundamental lesson about fire – fire is hot. A basic lesson.

I did not explain to him the varying temperatures related to the various colors of flame. We did not have a conversation about the process of combustion. The reason we didn't is obvious – he was not ready for that type of information.

God works with us in a similar way, here a little, there a little, God moves us from one level of revelation to the next level, from strength to strength, from faith to faith, from glory to glory – and this is the work of the Spirit.

WHEN I CAN'T FIND GOD

In like manner God's Truth is revealed by God progressively and is tailored to suit the needs of the person, time and place of the revelation. First, the milk of the Word of God, then the Meat, then the Strong Wine.

He was blind, legally blind, and couldn't see – other than shadows and dark images. He was deaf, legally deaf, and couldn't hear – other than muffled sounds and unintelligible noises. Nevertheless, he was in church every Sunday morning and every Sunday evening – like clockwork. He would stand when we sang and occasionally shout "Amen." as the Spirit came upon him.

One day I overheard someone shout a question to him [you had to shout for him to barely hear you]: "Brother Don, if you can't see the pastor behind the pulpit and if you can't hear the sermon when it's preached, why do you even come?"

"Why do I come," he asked loudly [and indignantly]? "I come so that the Devil will know WHERE I stand and WHO I stand with." Enough said. Thank you, Don.

Where do you stand? And, who do you stand with?

"Bulimia," says she. "I've had it for years and I've tried just about everything and been just about everywhere to get this monkey off my back. You're the end of the road for me. I have no where else to turn."

She described a long litany of inpatient and outpatient treatment centers, recovery programs, books she'd read, seminars she'd attended, and more –all to no avail.

A few things about her are etched in memory. First, I shared with her that her hope was in Christ and in Christ alone. Second, as her counseling progressed I gave her a written assignment. "Write a few brief sentences about each of the following, then add some concluding remarks: The Miracle Of Me, The Master Of Me, The Mystery Of Me and The Misery Of Me then Concluding Remarks."

She did that assignment, with an inordinate preoccupation that focused on "The Misery Of Me" with the following concluding sentence...

"Dear God, in misery, I am running away from You as fast as I can. Please catch me. Please."\

Anyone can run away from God – Jonah, Ezekiel and a host of others tried it -- without success. Jonah prayed to God from the belly of the fish, saying...

"I called out to the Lord,
out of my distress, and he answered me...."

Ezekiel, exhausted and in despair heard that special still voice of God while hiding in a cave.

Are you running from God? Many people try, but it's impossible. We simply can't run from an omnipresent God. It's impossible?

David indicated this when he wrote: "Where shall I go from your Spirit? Or where shall I flee from your presence? If I ascend to heaven, you are there. If I make my bed in Sheol, you are there. If I take the wings of the morning and dwell in the uttermost parts of the sea, even there your hand shall lead me, and your right hand shall hold me."

"Dear God, in misery, I am running away from You as fast as I can. Please catch me. Please."\

Some folks say "If I knew then what I know now." But, suppose we reverse that – "If I knew now what I knew then."

Memory is selective. It sorts and categories every event and every life experience – not haphazardly, nor with hesitation – but with intent and purpose. While cognitive intent and purpose vary, guided by many forces and governed by many factors – one primary purpose of the categorization is self-protection.

Self-protection extends beyond mere physical survival – and encompasses the emotional component as well. Sometimes, the avoidance of pain and the sting of self-confrontation are so strong that distortion occurs – and we reshape the events and life-experiences of the past. This is why the Bible warns us about the "deceitfulness" of man and the "deceitfulness" of the human heart.

The "deceitfulness" of man. Have you ever noticed that when you're reading a book or watching a movie – you always identify with the hero, the good guy, the guy who wins in the end. You don't see the villain as you – the villain simply is not and cannot be you. Why? Well, because he's a villain. The bad guy is not you either – the bad guy is not and cannot be you. Why? Well, because he's a bad guy. Me? A bad guy? Definitely not. Nope. Not me. I'm not the villain…I'm not the bad guy.

Now, think about this – then, the next time your mind acts like a television and you watch a "rerun" of a real life event or experience, the end of the story may be based more on what is now than what was back then when the event or life experience occurred.

Forgetfulness, by the way, is often an emotional tool that is used to minimize pain. Sometimes forgetfulness will even deny pains existence. We re-shuffle, then reshape events, then we watch our mental version of "what was" then we rerun that mental version again. We do this re-shuffle/re-shape/re-

WHEN I CAN'T FIND GOD

run again, and again, and again....

And, then, like the Prodigal Son who – came unto himself – we see the root of our misery – The Misery of Me – and we cry out to God...

"Dear God, in misery, I am running away from You as fast as I can. Please catch me. Please."

The old wooden house, surrounded by large southern Maple trees, was set back off of the dusty road. The place had that undeniable feel of history. Like an old relic from the past the house created that certain sense of nostalgic awe and wonder – awe and wonder about its better days and the people who once lived there. And now, well, the people who once lived there were gone. They had all died, one by one, except for one old man – a 79 yr. old bachelor -- Mr. Anthony.

An amazing wood burning, black pot-belly-stove sat between two huge windows, one on either side of a boarded up fireplace in the front room. Across the way, in the same room, was a bed, a single solitary quilt covered bed where Mr. Anthony slept. And, next to the bed sat Mr. Anthony, in an old rocking chair, rocking and creaking back and forth across a wooden floor. He wore an old, faded tee shirt under a pair of dusty overalls.

Mr. Hezzie Lloyd, my one deacon, introduced me to Mr. Anthony. I was the new pastor, just starting my ministry at my second church in the Village of Folsom, Louisiana. Mr. Anthony, Mr. Hezzie and I talked about many things that day.

"Sometimes I sit here and daydream about Ma-Ma and De-De," said Mr. Anthony, who had proudly finished the fourth grade at the now closed one room school house down the road. "When I was a boy all the old men sat around this here stove telling stories. And, now, well, I'm the old man but there aint nobody for me to tell my stories to..... Yes, sir, sometimes I sit here and daydream and I tell myself stories."

"Would you like to receive Jesus, Mr. Anthony? Would you like to invite Christ into your heart?"

He stopped rocking, looked intently at me, as one man looking to another man, eye to eye, with a silent stare. "Yes," said Mr. Anthony with a tear in the corners of his eyes. "I would like to do that."

We knelt down, holding hands, forming a circle, Mr. Hezzie, Mr. Anthony and me, as Mr. Anthony invited Christ into his life. Mr. Anthony turned away from Something (his Sin) and turned toward Someone (his Savior). He was saved, born-again, and excited about it too.

"Anthony," asked Mr. Hezzie. "I've been visiting and visiting you for nearly 40 yrs. I've come with preacher after preacher and haven't been able to get you to church – not one time, that I can recall, not one time. Today, I come with this here young preacher boy and bammmm you invite Jesus into your life. I don't understand – what's different this time?"

"Well, those others asked me to go to church. This fella asked me to invite Jesus in my life. I kinda reckon that's what I needed all along – Jesus in my life."

The following Sunday Mr. Anthony made a public profession of faith and was baptized and, he attended church faithfully, Sunday after Sunday until his untimely death six years later.

"I kinda reckon that's what I needed all along – Jesus in my life."

> And, who is it that has been and is waiting for you,
> Just for you
> Like an old mother hen?

WHEN I CAN'T FIND GOD

Encouragers
Special Thanks to the Encouragers listed below
for their financial and prayer support

Anonymous Memorial Gift in
Memory of my father, Cosmas Jeffries

Doris Jeffries
Cosmas Sean Jeffries
Sheri Jeffries Bankson
Courtney Jeffries Geoperopolis
Glenn and Linda Jeffries
TerryAnn Fielding
Scott and Cathy Jeffries
Mark and Kelly bates
Elizabeth J Clark
John C Tucker Sr
Laurie Flanagan
Cathy Denning
Nancy Brashear Ford
Malynda Guarisco
Shannon Nevels
Jake and Kim Schiro
Tina Schiro
Cory Shaw
Elyn Walker

DR JOHN DEE JEFFRIES

WHEN I CAN'T FIND GOD

www.ingramcontent.com/pod-product-compliance
Lightning Source LLC
Chambersburg PA
CBHW032044290426
44110CB00012B/942